Savvy
SENIOR SINGLES

to Marge —
God bless you on
your journey !   Samantha

Savvy
SENIOR SINGLES

Navigating the Singles' World from 50 and Beyond

Samantha Landy

DESTINY IMAGE® PUBLISHERS, INC.

P.O. Box 310, Shippensburg, PA 17257-0310

"Speaking to the Purposes of God for this Generation and for the Generations to Come."

This book and all other Destiny Image, Revival Press, Mercy Place, Fresh Bread, Destiny Image Fiction, and Treasure House books are available at Christian bookstores and distributors worldwide.

For a U.S. bookstore nearest you, call 1-800-722-6774.
For more information on foreign distributors, call 717-532-3040.
Or reach us on the Internet: **www.destinyimage.com.**

ISBN 10: 0-7684-2409-7
ISBN 13: 978-0-7684-2409-6

For Worldwide Distribution, Printed in the U.S.A.

1 2 3 4 5 6 7 8 9 10 11 / 09 08 07 06

DEDICATION

To my Lord Jesus Christ,
whose overwhelming love, joy, peace,
and mercy made this book possible.

ACKNOWLEDGEMENTS

Through the years our lives crisscross with many people, each one leaving a deposit in our hearts. It is impossible for me to mention all who have touched my life, as this book is a composite of many lives and many stories. As I wrote in the beginning chapter, this book is by Savvy Singles and for Savvy Singles. However, the following is a list of people to whom I am most indebted.

I owe deep gratitude to Cecil Murphey, author of over 90 books, writing instructor, who challenged me to excellence. Greg Griffith often shared Scriptures of encouragement with me, prayed with me, and spurred me on to fulfill my dreams. Dee Simmons who with her sweet Texas drawl opened doors of opportunity for me because she, too, believed in my project. Dorree Sullivan who kept things organized in my life while I concentrated on my writing. Bradley James, a dreamer of dreams who pushed me into fulfilling mine.

Cheryl Prewitt Salem, Miss America 1980, it's been your warm counsel that has often given me light for the next step. Timothy and Hazel Starr from Toronto, Canada, your belief in me and your phone calls of encouragement always came on the day I needed them. Joe Mijich, an attorney friend from Seattle, who enthusiastically provided some of the material for the chapter on Prenuptial Agreements. My four sisters and brother, Bob, and Winona, my sister-in-law. Winona, it has been your statement from years ago that kept me plodding on, "Samantha, the world needs this book!" My good friends on the board of Christian Celebrity Luncheons, Gwen Schoonover, Beverly Jackson, Dorree Sullivan, Mona Rae Miller, Geri Dotson, Suzy Jones, and Rosemary Hartman: Thanks. You have always been my biggest fans and strongest prayer warriors.

Finally, a special thanks to my two sons, Jim and Randy. It has been a privilege and joy to be your mom and watch you grow up into such fine young men, full of integrity and enthusiasm. A special thanks to my five grandchildren—Jim, Ramsey, Katie, Brandi, and Shawn—you've been wonderful sources of inspiration for many of my stories. The value you all add to my life is immeasurable. I love you with all of my heart.

ENDORSEMENTS

Samantha really is her book. She has discovered secrets that she has lived out to a great degree of success. The real life stories she has woven into her book will capture the interest of both women and men since we both have experienced virtually the same things. She certainly captured my interest. It great to know—and to learn—we can really be smart about living at any age. You'll enjoy reading this book.

Oral Roberts
Pastor, Evangelist, Author

I like books that really are on target for the express needs of a particular group of people, they are pointed and powerful. Samantha Landy is a savvy person with a profound faith and a practical application of biblical truth for singles, particularly in the 50+ generations. This is a contemporary, no-nonsense, honest, and extremely sensitive book that deals with real issues. Reading this book will help you find God's answers to your deepest questions and most urgent concerns. I highly recommend *Savvy Senior Singles*.

Dr. Lloyd Ogilvie
Retired Chaplain of the U.S. Senate

"Where do I go from here?" This question is on the minds of millions of individuals who find themselves sleeping single in a double-bed for one reason or another. The words "lonely" and "single" don't necessarily go together. Whether you are single by choice or by fate, *Savvy Senior Singles* not only will help you learn to face the reality of this state of being, it will point the way to the type of Bible-based savvy living that can produce happiness, fulfillment, and satisfaction.

Tom Harken
Entrepreneur, Horatio Alger Award Recipient

Inspired by her own navigation of the single world after she was widowed, Samantha Landy has captured the essence of being single for the 50+ set. This wonderful book is filled with humor and stories that will delight you and offers beneficial information to any senior, single or married.

Patti & Gavin MacLeod
TV Personality: The Love Boat Captain

Every savvy single needs the wisdom, the insight, and the humor of *Savvy Senior Singles* for the deep needs of the single's heart, so beautifully expressed in this book. I highly recommend it.

Rhonda Fleming Carlson
Actress, Philanthropist, Humanitarian

No one I've met is better qualified than Samantha Landy to guide our generation into becoming *Savvy Singles*. In this special book, *Savvy Senior Singles*, she speaks to us with elegance and wisdom, prescribing belief in ourselves through belief in God.

Louise DuArt, Comedic Impressionist
Host, "Living the Life," ABC Family Channel

This wonderful book, *Savvy Senior Singles*, is a brilliant roadmap for "boomovers"—those of us who have zoomed past the equator of life, toward what Samantha Landy calls "our best years"...those years that God has appropriately saved for last.

SQuire Rushnell
Author, *When God Winks* and
When God Winks on Love

I hold Samantha Landy as a dear friend, personally and professionally. I've seen firsthand what she has overcome as a married woman and as a single lady through the many trials in life. I believe her writing gift, including *Savvy Senior Singles*, Navigating the Singles' World, can inspire many to continue in life and never give up. You'll love this book.

Cheryl Salem, Miss America 1980
Minister, Author, and Musician

After a wonderful marriage of 25 years, Samantha's husband died and she began navigating a new, uncharted journey in her life. She trusted God to guide her and found that there were many 50+ singles who also didn't have experience living the single life. Out of this awareness, *Savvy Senior Singles* was born. Destined to be a best seller, *Savvy Senior Singles* will not only delight the reader, but offers insight into how to live in today's 50+ singles' world.

Greg Griffith
President and CEO, G&G Global Development, Inc.

Finally, a book for singles not afraid to tell the truth. Samantha Landy's book, *Savvy Senior Singles*, goes straight to the heart of crucial singles' issues for men and women of the 50+ set. From her own experiences and careful observation, Samantha bravely delves into areas facing singles with sensitivity, research, practicality, and humor that few authors will attempt. It is a realistic guide for healthier, more dynamic relationships that will change your life.

Bradley James
Speaker and Composer, Producer,
Performer of "Gift of Love: Music to the Words and Prayers of Mother Teresa"

Once again, Samantha Landy has written a book expressly to meet the needs of her audience. *Savvy Senior Singles*, consistently applies timeless truths about how to live a fulfilled, exciting life from 50 and beyond, based on her favorite book of all time, the Bible. Some of her stories will make you laugh or even cry, but applying the principles she has written about, will indeed encourage you on your own road to becoming a Savvy Single. You'll want your friends to have this book too!

Michael Ray Smith, Ph.D.
Campbell University Chair,
Department of Mass Communication

Samantha Landy is a wordsmith and storyteller. She does this through speaking, teaching, writing or counseling. She takes words and leads her listeners and readers to say: "I never quite thought of it that way before." *Savvy Senior Singles* is a superb document giving down-to-earth practical hints for singles in every aspect of living. From her own background, she shares significant insight in all aspects of singleness. I am recommending this volume to all singles without any reservations. It is bound to have a positive impact on your life.

Timothy Starr (D'M), Toronto, Canada
Pastor to Singles and Single Again,
The Peoples Church
President, Christian Seniors in Action

TABLE OF CONTENTS

FOREWORD

A single senior? How do you *choose* to spend these years? In loneliness, isolation, hopelessness; or love, joy, and peace?

Choices...we all have them. We make them each day, and each one ushers in its own realities. Right ones bring hope for a brighter tomorrow. Fulfilling relationships, meaningful acts of service; consciously allowing God's spirit to radiate through us. Enjoying a beautiful life passage through which our spiritual discernment blossoms as it could never do in our younger years.

Choices...we all have them.

This helpful book, written by a God-loving, beautiful spirit, can guide you through these times when natural life-changing transitions are removing old friends and family one by one; and your relationship options seem to be lessening. The insights shared by the author can help you set new, exciting goals, renew your hope, and prepare you for the Savior who now awaits you, and is prepared to change your lowly body into the likeness of His glorious one.

But I must warn you. Simply reading this book and putting it aside will do you little good. Instead, get a pen or highlighter and slowly digest your way through it. Take action on this godly person's ideas. For it is through your choices and their resulting actions that you will open the door to a fulfilling now—joyously looking forward to that commonwealth that awaits us as God's children.

Choices...we all have them.

Choose now to spend these wonderful senior years lavishing in the abundant blessings that God provides for you...His child.

Ron Willingham
Founder and CEO, Integrity Systems

SECTION ONE:

It's All About Us

INTRODUCTION

What is a Savvy Senior Single?

Savvy: Well informed and perceptive; practical understanding or shrewdness.

Senior: Being in a position above others; being the older; having precedence in making certain decisions.

Single: Not accompanied by another; consisting of one part; individual and distinct.

Section One is all about us. It's about intelligent people over 50 years of age who are unmarried. It's about our attitudes, our choices, and about deciding who we really want to be for the rest of our lives. What does being a Savvy Single really mean? Together we will search our hearts, our goals, and our dreams; and then discover the answer.

The following poem sums up this first section of the book very well. It was sent to me by a good friend, Sue, who is a Savvy Single living out her dreams and dreaming new ones.

Someone will always be prettier.
Someone will always be smarter.

Her house will be bigger.
She will drive a better car.
Her children will do better in school,
And her husband will fix more
things around the house.
So let it go, and love you
and your circumstances.
Think about it.

The prettiest woman in the world
can have hatred in her heart.
And the most highly favored
Woman at your church may be
unable to have children.

And the richest woman you know,

Who has the car, the house,
the clothes...might be lonely.

And the Bible says if I "do not
have love I am nothing."

So again, love you.
Love who you are.

Introduction

*Look in the mirror in the
morning and smile and say,*

*"I am too blessed to be stressed,
and too anointed to be disappointed!"*

*To the world you might
be just one person,*

*but to one person you just
might be the world.*

(Author unknown)

This true-to-life poem, while written for women (maybe we obsess more?), also applies to men. There will always be another man who is more handsome, thinner, more successful with bigger toys. We all need to focus on God and who God wants to be in our lives. So read on, dear friends, let's start navigating the waters of the singles' world together.

Chapter 1

SO WE'RE SINGLE

Oh! Teach us to live well! Teach us to live wisely and well! ...Surprise us with love at daybreak; then we'll skip and dance all day long ...And let the loveliness of the Lord, our God, rest on us, confirming the work that we do. Oh yes. Affirm the work that we do!
Psalm 90:12-17 (TM)

This Scripture passage truly sets the tone of this book. My hope is that it will help you to gracefully navigate through the uncharted waters of being 50+ in a singles' world.

I believe that a truly Savvy Senior Single isn't looking for another self-help book that promises a fantastic new body for anyone who follows a mile-long list of impossible rules and expensive regimens. I guarantee that isn't what this book is about. I hope that doesn't disappoint you.

If you're like me, you've had it with empty promises and unfulfilled expectations. Most often such promises are presented by people who don't have a clue about what it's like to walk in the shoes of a single living in a world that idolizes youth and denies the validity of the natural aging process.

That's exactly why I felt compelled to write this book. It's a book about helping—helping Savvy Singles not only with practical issues such as how to protect against identity theft or venereal disease; but also about helping process the emotional, mental, and spiritual issues we grapple with on a daily basis.

I believe the most important key to living successfully as a Savvy Single is to have a personal relationship with the Lord Jesus Christ. Therefore, the standard by which decisions should be weighed is the Bible—the greatest guidebook of all time.

The world in which we live is very different from biblical days. Therefore, we are faced with many challenges never even imagined in apostle Paul's day, when the family cared for widows and divorce was a rare. Today, divorce is rampant in our society; and the family unit no longer includes multiple generations under one roof. Families are scattered geographically so when death or divorce occurs during the senior years, men and women are suddenly thrust into a strange and lonely world of singleness.

The moral culture of our time has declined significantly in many ways—including Internet pornography and sexually-transmitted diseases—putting vulnerable senior singles at risk and even in danger. I realize that portions of the subject matter presented may be uncomfortable for some readers.

However, the purpose of the book is to discuss real issues facing real people in today's society. My intent is to provide sound biblical principles to empower senior singles to maximize their lives with joy and success. If you don't agree with something you read, please submit it to the Lord in prayer and allow Him to give you direction.

If you're not single and reading this book, that's OK. If you are over 50 years of age, it is very possible you may be faced with living as a single in the years ahead. The majority of us have had singleness thrust upon us through the death of a spouse or perhaps through divorce, but we are seldom prepared to live alone. My hope is that the insights and experiences shared within this book will help prepare you for such a time.

Although many of us don't want to be referred to as "seniors," those of us in the "50+ Set" who are single have very real and unique issues to deal with on a daily basis. I choose to refer to our group as "Savvy Singles."

DEFINING US

While researching for this book, I found that the word *seniors* has become difficult to define regarding who is included in that group. Being single, on the other hand, is easily defined. It's like being pregnant—either you are or you aren't. But here is my dilemma in identifying the senior single group.

In the June 2006 issue of *Significant Living* Magazine author Jerry Rose wrote, "Every seven seconds in America someone is turning 50 years old and is facing the second half of life. In the next five years 11,000 people a day will turn fifty. It is a demographic explosion unprecedented in American history." As we enter the age of being a senior, whether through divorce or death, nearly half of us will be a senior single.

Scripture tells us that Paul instructs Timothy about how the church is to make provision for widows. In First Timothy 5:9, Paul refers to widows who are over 60 as those who could be placed on a list for the church to assist. Perhaps 60 is the senior age standard that makes the most sense even today. With people living longer, I've heard it said that "50 is the new 40."

However, for marketing purposes many organizations are pushing the senior qualifying age down rather than up. The American Association for Retired People (AARP) magazine now includes people 50 and over as a senior. Features have included Oprah Winfrey's 50th birthday celebration, along with Christie Brinkley, John Travolta, and Patty Hearst, all of whom turned 50 in January and February 2004.

Now, this is where the definition of being a senior gets fuzzy. Unlike AARP's 50 and above definition, in order to qualify for the senior discount at Borders bookstore, you must be 65 years of age—the same for Barnes and Noble, at least in our area.

Most movie theatres around the country allow you to buy a senior ticket if you look like, or can prove you are 55. My friend Lorie and I decided to go to the 5:15 P.M. movie at a local theatre. Being early, we were the only ones standing in line. When the young man came to the ticket window, as usual I requested a senior ticket for the movie we were planning to see.

"You have to be fifty-five to buy a senior ticket," he said, as he studied me.

"That's fine, I'm over fifty-five."

He stared at me for a moment and then said, "I'll have to see your driver's license." It surprised me and I decided to tease him a little.

"You really don't need to see my driver's license," I replied, "I really am over fifty-five. Here's my money." Then I turned to Lorie and said, "Can you imagine, he wants to see my driver's license!" She just smiled.

By this time, the young man was certain that I was trying to get away with something and quite loudly said, "Ma'am, you'll have to show me your driver's license or pay the full price!"

This prompted his manager to come over to check out this woman who was trying to cheat the theatre out of a full-price ticket. After a bit more joking on my part, I finally showed them my license. Without a word, the young man punched the senior ticket price into the cash register and took my money. They didn't see any humor in being wrong. Lorie and I giggled all evening about being "carded" at the movies.

Many of us would prefer not to admit being a senior, let alone a senior single. That is why I've coined the term *Savvy Singles*. We do, however, like the senior discounts. I guess it doesn't really matter at what point we decide to cross that line and join the ranks of the senior generation—we all do it sooner or later.

I thought of having this book published with a simple brown paper cover with no title on it so no one would know you were buying a book for seniors; but my publisher didn't agree.

"How would they find it on the shelf?" he asked.

"Simple," I replied, "It would be the only untitled book with a brown paper cover!"

My humor didn't convince him so as you walked up to the counter to pay for this book, everyone you passed and the young sales person knows you are a Savvy Single in the 50+ set, a.k.a. a senior. Of course you could have explained that you were buying it for your mother.

ONE IS A WHOLE NUMBER

Being single doesn't mean we are deficient or lacking in life. Will we ever learn that singleness does *not* mean we are defective? Being single doesn't mean that we are less than. Less than what? Less than whole? Less than complete? It's critical that you settle this one truth in your mind right now—One is a whole number!

Learning to flourish where you are and how to thrive in your current situation are essential to preparing for new opportunities that will come your way. To do this you must stop looking at your past and start looking toward your future. Now is the perfect time to redefine who you are, who you want to be, and where you want to go. This is an exciting time in your life.

If there is any doubt in your mind whether you are whole and complete as a Savvy Single, meditate on this Scripture, *"Now thanks be to God who always leads us in triumph in*

Christ, and through us diffuses the fragrance of His knowl-
edge in every place" (2 Cor. 2:14 NKJV). This is a promise
that as we breathe in the knowledge of God's Word, He will
help us triumph in our lives as Savvy Singles. It doesn't say
we will triumph if we are a couple. It simply says God always leads *"us"*—single or married—to triumph in Christ.

After experiencing a setback like divorce or the death of a
spouse, the most important step to consider is how to make
a comeback. Finding someone else to marry is not necessarily the first order of business.

God knows exactly where you are. Here is a promise to
ponder in your heart: *"'For I know the plans I have for you,'*
declares the LORD, 'plans to prosper you and not to harm
you, plans to give you hope and a future'" (Jer. 29:11 NIV).

My own life is a testimony that God has a plan for each of
us. Even though I received Christ into my heart at 5 1/2 years
of age and felt very close to Jesus as a child, I became rebel-
lious in my teens and early twenties and married a man my
parents didn't want me to marry. For a few years I thought we
were happy, but when I found myself divorced, though not of
my own choosing, I became angry with men as well as God.

Some years later, I decided to study Zen Buddhism. Then
I took classes on astrology and tarot cards and went on an
ESP weekend. What my friends and I were doing was seeking the ultimate truth—seeking nirvana—always seeking
but never finding it.

One night during those years of searching and frustration, I knelt by my chair and recommitted my life to Christ.
The incredible joy I felt that night brought back memories

of my salvation as a child. I knew I had found the Ultimate Truth in Christ. I had been vainly searching for it in all the wrong places.

Only a few months later, through circumstances only God could have arranged, I met Morry, a man who had been a Christian for about two years. God blessed us with a wonderful, memorable marriage. We ministered together in many venues for 25 years before he went home to Heaven. God had my future in His hand all along.

After Morry died, I began a journey as a single person on a road I had not traveled before. During the day, I was usually okay. I kept very busy, but loneliness stalked me relentlessly. I found myself awakening in the night with tears running down my cheeks. My mind became my enemy as I let it drift back, over and over into the memories of our wonderful marriage and the pain of my loss.

Sometimes I thought it would have been easier had we not liked, as well as loved, each other. We were very compatible, playing golf together, enjoying the same interests and the same friends. But most of all we enjoyed each other. It was a good, as well as godly, marriage. So when he died, I missed him. I missed our afternoon cup of tea together. I longed for those times of companionship on the golf course or simply watching a beautiful sunset. Death is so final.

One morning I realized I had to stop concentrating on what I had lost and begin being thankful for what I still possessed. I had good health. I had two wonderful sons and five little grandchildren. I still had my four sisters and my brother. I had many friends. I had a roof over my head, food to eat, and clothes to wear. As I began to make an attitude adjustment that day, I found myself on the path to my comeback.

A couple of years ago, I heard Dr. Lloyd Ogilvie, retired Chaplain of the U.S. Senate, speak at a small group in Beverly Hills at the home of my good friend, Rhonda Fleming Carlson. At one point in his talk he mentioned how lonely his life is since his beloved Mary Jane died. "I learned gratitude is the antidote to grief," Dr. Ogilvie said, "I sat down and began to thank God for His goodness to me. The moment one definitely commits to an attitude of gratitude, then Providence moves in to mend our broken lives." And so it is.

COMEBACKS AND DRAWBACKS

Sometimes we are so busy longing to be one of the "couples," we forget that there are advantages to being single. For instance, it isn't necessary to ask if it is okay to go shopping with our friends. If we want to buy something new, we don't have to ask for anyone else's input or approval. If we don't like the blood and violence of war movies, we can find a tearjerker, romance film and go with a friend. As a married couple, it is only natural to consider what our spouse might want. But as a single person, we are basically free to do whatever we want to do whenever we want to do it.

However, on any given "cold and stormy night," being single doesn't seem to be an advantage. While I am not above allowing myself a little pity party now and then, I've found there are some things we can learn during this part of our journey too.

Many times, we take things way too seriously, including our friendships. Learning to approach meeting a new person with the idea of making a great friend rather than immediately wondering if this person would be good marriage material is important. As we encounter new relationships, our friendships will be more fulfilling. It is a joy to get to know the opposite sex as friends before considering a lifetime commitment.

One of my favorite authors, Mike Murdock, writes in his book, *101 Wisdom Keys*, "The worth of any relationship can be measured by its contributions to your priorities." In his writings, he suggests we evaluate every person in our life by writing, "Every relationship in your life is a current moving you toward your dreams or away from them."

As a Savvy Single, we need to keep those statements as a priority in our minds when considering our relationships with the people in our lives. Ask yourself, "Does this person encourage me to pursue my dreams or try to draw me away from them?"

One of the benefits of being a Savvy Single is that we can network with many different people who can make significant contributions in our lives. We can learn something from everyone, including teenagers and children.

King Solomon, the wisest man who ever lived, wrote, *"The mind of the prudent is ever getting knowledge; and the ear of the wise is ever seeking—inquiring and craving—knowledge"* (Prov. 18:15 AMP). Often we have a need for the knowledge of others at a particular moment in time. If we develop a large circle of friends and acquaintances, chances are, when we need information, we'll know someone to ask.

Greg, a good friend of mine from Florida, often asks how my latest book is coming along. Since he is more skilled on the Internet than I am, he offers to help with on-line research when I need it. He is also a professional at marketing and gives me advice in this area too. This is a friend who is helping me toward my dreams. He is valued as someone who offers to share his gifts and talents.

I also am fortunate to have a dear friend locally, Georgeann, who helps me with computer problems. Bradley is another friend with whom I have great discussions about ancient religions, music, goal setting, and so on. Dee, my friend who owns Ultimate Living,™ keeps me healthy with her healthy vitamins and nutritious drinks. While I have many other friends, I mention these few to give you an idea about why it's good to have a variety of friends—friends who help us toward our dreams. Hopefully, I am the kind of friend they need as well.

To be successful as a Savvy Single, it's also important to listen to others. Everyone hears through a different frame of reference, and sometimes we need a paradigm shift in perspective to take us to where we want to be. Someone in your life knows something you need to know, but you will not discover it until you stop and listen.

One piece of information can turn a failure into a success. The definition of success as a Savvy Single is our own choice. But success at whatever level we choose still takes work. Henry Wadsworth Longfellow put it this way, "Some people succeed because they are destined to, but most people succeed because they are determined to!" Determination is an important asset we need to develop on our road to success as a Savvy Single.

WHY?

When a friend asked me why I was writing this book, I didn't hesitate for a second to answer; I had been thinking about it for some time. Since becoming a Savvy Single, I've looked for books that would help me deal with the various issues I was experiencing. I couldn't find any. There were, however, many books written for singles in the 30-to-50 age brackets.

This is not a book about analyzing and defining the idiosyncrasies of singles, like some scientist writing deep in some dark basement studying the life cycle of a butterfly. Not on your life! This is a book written to and by Savvy Singles whose stories give this book substance.

For years I have collected stories from people across the country. To protect their privacy, I have changed the names, cities, and other pertinent information. So, if a story is similar to that of someone you know, don't worry, it's not. Although God created us as unique individuals, at some levels we all have similar life stories, don't we?

The following chapters will help you make wise decisions about your everyday practical living circumstances. But the main thrust of this book is to help us all learn to successfully live with reality and wisdom in the situation we're in now. That's what defines a Savvy Single.

Our circumstances may not immediately change, but changing our attitudes will make all the difference in the world. We can make the decision to have joy in our lives no matter what issues we face, because *"the joy of the Lord is your strength"* (Neh. 8:10). Some of the stories may make you laugh or some may make you cry, some may even make you angry at the situations we allow to impact our lives.

Being single at a mature age often requires learning to do things a new way. Even simple things like walking into a meeting alone, going to church alone, or going to a movie alone are different as a single person. In the coming chapters we will explore many new ways of thinking and doing things as a Savvy Single.

Being a Savvy Single is about learning to dream again! The world still loves dreamers, no matter what age. Let's learn and dream together as we navigate through the world of a Savvy Single in the twenty-first century.

Perhaps the best thing to learn about success as a Savvy Single is that you can have joy in your life, right where you are. All it takes is a little attitude adjustment and adopting some new rules of the road to maximize your life as a Savvy Single.

POINTS TO PONDER

❖ Weigh your decisions by the Bible.

❖ Being single is easily identifiable—being a senior isn't as clear according to today's society.

❖ One is a whole number!

❖ Take time to redefine who you are, who you want to be, and where you want to go.

❖ "The moment one definitely commits to an attitude of gratitude, then Providence moves in to mend our broken lives." Dr. Lloyd Ogilvie

❖ Networking with a variety of people makes significant contributions in your life.

❖ Determination is an important asset to success as a Savvy Single.

❖ Changing your attitude will make all the difference in the world.

❖ Being single at a mature age often requires learning to do things a new way.

Chapter 2

"IT TAKES A LONG TIME TO GROW YOUNG"

How in the world did this happen? Did I fall asleep, like Rip Van Winkle, and not notice when I woke up that I was 20 years older? Those are the questions I sometimes ask myself about becoming a Savvy Single. I like Pablo Picasso's view on life when he said, "It takes a long time to grow young." That's what I aim for—to grow young.

In one of my old flip-over calendars I came across this profound statement by an unnamed author:

You are as young as your faith, as old as your doubt;
as young as your self-confidence, as old as your fear;
as young as your hope, as old as your despair.

That's worth reading again.

It makes us really stop and think, doesn't it?

There are more of "us" every day. Currently, there are more than 78 million Americans over the age of 50. And every seven seconds someone in the United States turns 55, a trend that will continue for the next 15 years.

Maybe getting older isn't as important as how we handle it. Getting older is inevitable, but how we handle our doubts, fears, and despair makes a monumental difference whatever our age.

Of course, refusing to go into that "senior citizen" season is pretty hard when AARP keeps sending me messages and insurance companies keep reminding me that I need to make prearrangements for my funeral!

"Live your life and forget your age," Dr. Norman Vincent Peale thundered from his pulpit at the Marble Collegiate Church in New York City one Sunday morning. Dr. Peale, known for his positive thinking concepts also encouraged spontaneity in life. He lived into his mid-90s and was known for impulsively stopping whatever he was doing to encourage someone or listen to their needs.

Like most of us, my Daily Planner lists events that I've committed to a year in advance. But it's essential to leave lots of white space on our calendars for impromptu, serendipitous events or invitations. We never know what delightful surprises might come our way, on any given day, if we leave time for them. It is a malady of our times; we're always in a rush, often not sure why or where we're going or when we'll get there.

An unplanned lunch with a friend could turn into a life-changing event. A solitary walk in the park could restore and refresh your soul. Attempting the unfamiliar could open new horizons of creativity.

JUST BECAUSE

Spontaneity is an attitude that keeps us young. When we watch small children play, it's not unusual for them to switch from one activity to the other without hesitation, just enjoying the freedom of the moment. When we're young, we are spontaneous, but as we grow older, we allow our busyness to squelch the joy of impulse out of our lives.

"It takes a long time to grow young." Let Picasso's statement resonate in your heart. To rephrase his statement, "We're never too old to have a second childhood!" For instance, when was the last time you went sledding, built sandcastles, or enjoyed some other childhood fun?

I have fond memories of a spur-of-the-moment activity I experienced some years ago while skiing with friends in Lake Tahoe. We stayed at the Inn on the Truckee River. It was an incredible place owned by an Austrian who claimed to be a Count. Many photographs on the restaurant walls pictured him with Queen Elizabeth, other notables, actresses, and actors.

During dinner the second night, huge snowflakes began falling. We had been skiing all day but after dinner one of my friends, Ralph, suggested he and I go out walking in the falling snow.

Just outside the door snow covered a large flat lawn area. Suddenly, I had the urge to make a snow angel like I used to do when I was a kid.

Ralph was laughing as I flopped down on my back in the snow and started waving my arms up and down. I asked him if he had ever made a snow angel. Growing up in the San Francisco Bay Area, he had not. I convinced him to lie down in the snow and make an angel too. People watched us out the large restaurant windows overlooking the river, pointing and laughing along with us.

We finished our snow angels, merrily brushing off the snow. Shortly, the owner came out, bringing us mugs of hot chocolate. The three of us sat at one of the outdoor tables talking as we watched the snow pile up on the rocks out in the dark, flowing river. With the full moon and the sound of the rushing river, those were magical, memorable moments.

It's been too long since I made those snow angels. Maybe for most of us, it's been too long for lots of simple, wondrous things that used to give us joy as children. Walking the beach in the early morning fog; lying on the grass and watching a ladybug crawl across our finger; stopping to listen to the meadowlark's song; gathering a bouquet of dandelions to put on the kitchen window sill—these and a myriad of other simple pleasures will help us grow young. Learning to grow young is a choice we must make and can experience at any moment.

THE SECRET?

One day, I happened to be standing in front of the sliding mirrored closet door in my bedroom as I put on hand lotion. Rubbing the lotion around the cuticles as Mom used to remind me, suddenly I thought, all of my life I have hated my long fingers and hands. Now that I'm finally keeping them manicured and soft, I see maybe they really are fine.

In recent years people have told me I have lovely hands, and I've begun to believe them, maybe I do. Idly, I wondered what other distorted ideas I have had about myself from when I was young.

When I was growing up, some parents (including mine) didn't compliment their children. I guess they thought the children might become prideful. Like many youngsters then and today, I started to believe that there wasn't much good about my body. I thought I was too tall and skinny. Being taller than most of the boys in school, I hunched my shoulders, which exacerbated the disapproval of Mom. Now there is the TV mythical image portrayed by all the young actors and actresses that makes us feel not only old, but obviously out of shape. As we get older, it's easy to degrade ourselves, forgetting we never did look like Julia Roberts or George Clooney. I admit to a little sense of delicious revenge when I see an older performer who hasn't aged all that well either!

The suave dancer, Fred Astaire said, "Old age is like everything else, to make a success of it, you've got to start young." He certainly kept his grace, elegance, and stamina throughout his career, often dancing with women many years younger.

What is the secret to successful aging? Is it exercise? Nutrition? Good genes? Healthy relationships? All four are of consequence. However, too often we don't realize that quality relationships also help us stay healthy and age gracefully.

When we were young, often we assumed that "special someone" had to be a spouse, and only after we were married would we be fulfilled. But as we get older and single again, or still single, we can choose to develop a few close friends to fill our need for companionship.

While I agree that close friends are important, as I get older, I also enjoy having many friends and acquaintances with whom to participate in various activities of particular interest. The variety of activities adds zest to my life.

When we become single again, regardless the reason, it's hard to imagine not being a couple—then suddenly the whole world seems to be made up of couples. Even the cruise industry caters to couples; a single has to pay extra for taking up a whole room!

I discovered how Esther, a new friend I met on a cruise to Alaska, copes with being single. She wistfully told me how she and her husband loved to dance and went dancing almost every weekend. Her spouse has been deceased many years but that hasn't stopped Esther from being optimistic and upbeat.

So what did she do with her beloved dancing partner gone? She began organizing dance groups of retired people where she lives.

Esther is over 80 years of age but still enjoys cruises with a girl friend, and dances all evening with the dance hosts that the cruise ship supplies. On the Alaskan cruise when we met, the dance hosts were much younger than Esther, but they enjoyed dancing with her not only because of her vivacity for life and animated personality, but she was an excellent dancer as well.

I was relating this story to a friend of mine, Cecil, who said, "As a dancer myself, it's such joy to dance with any woman—regardless of age—who can follow well." Makes me want to work on my dance steps!

Esther makes daily choices to keep her joy in spite of the normal aches and pains of being 80. Each day, for her, is filled with excitement. She put as much energy and enthusiasm into playing the trivia contests as she did dancing. She refused to be limited by age, loving every moment of life. That's the secret of a Savvy Single.

Aging is a life-long process and how well we do it is up to each one of us.

After making the movie, "Grumpy Old Men," Jack Lemmon and Walter Matthau said in an interview that they had as much fun clowning around on the TV set as they said they did making the movie. Even though they were in the later stages of their lives, they chose to keep their sense of humor. Their waggish banter kept them interesting and young.

INSIDE OUT

One day when I was a little girl sitting on my Grandma's front porch, she said, "Now, don't tell anyone or they'll think I'm crazy, but while I know I'm almost seventy, sometimes I feel nineteen in my mind." At the time, I did think she was a little crazy. As I become older, I too feel young at heart and now I understand her.

"Inside every seventy year old is a thirty five year old asking, what happened?" This is a similar idea expressed by newspaper advice columnist Ann Landers.

Appearance, health, and circumstances change with time and often without our permission or approval. Many people cope with the stress of aging by dressing younger or erasing age lines. When this is done in moderation and good taste, it can indeed improve our outward appearance and perhaps our confidence.

Yet, I've found that the people who are the most engaging and sought after for friendships are those who choose to keep a young spirit, a young attitude about life. They're people who love to embrace the world around them, retain that sparkle in their eye and exuberance in their walk, in spite of unplanned and difficult events in their lives.

I've been fortunate to know many people who have faced life in their senior years, with grace, humility, and humor. I've even known a few who have embraced life and aging with great gusto. They are exciting to be around.

How do you face life? Is the glass half full or half empty? Are you optimistic or pessimistic?

A good friend, Odette, who is totally blind and lives in the San Francisco area, said just the other night, "We need to be thankful for what we have and not whine about what we don't have."

Actually, Odette is one of my unmarried heroines and has been my friend for over 30 years. She is French, tiny, with steel gray hair and is in her 90s. Odette's father was the French Ambassador to China so she lived in China from the time she was 2 years old until she was 22 when they returned to France just before World War II. In her later years, she became a writer, chronicling much of her amazing life as well as writing a devotional book, both in French and English.

Although she became blind 20 years ago, she still lives alone and is very determined to do so. Even in her years of blindness, she sends a monthly cassette tape to her sister in France who lives in a Catholic retirement home and is also blind.

Why is sending the cassette tape remarkable? She has trained herself, using two tape recorders, to translate various teaching tapes, sentence by sentence from English into French.

Without her sight, she must remember which buttons and knobs to push. And which ones she just pushed! Her tenacity not only to survive, but to choose to give purpose and meaning to her life in the most difficult of circumstances is remarkable. This puts her high up on my pedestal of incredible women and Savvy Single role models.

I'm not implying she is a Pollyanna. On the contrary, she's had her share of sleepless nights, wondering what she should do, and what will happen to her. Yet she isn't sitting around bemoaning her fate. She's chosen to be passionate and creative with her life.

Isn't there something exciting about enthusiastic people who don't moan, groan, or grump but see life as something terrific, filled with opportunity and choices?

Are we able to adapt when life throws us a curve? Do we choose to learn from each circumstance? Or do we just react to events and situations. We can choose to create meaning and purpose in our lives that transcend our stressful events.

Recently, while going through a painful event in my life, I had to speak at a luncheon meeting in the San Francisco area of California. Numerous friends were at the luncheon. A lady who knew of my circumstances, came up to me and said, "Oh you poor dear, you look like a little wounded bird."

My first thought was that perhaps my stress showed more than I thought or maybe I hadn't put on my makeup very well. Then I realized that was just her personality, not mine.

"Really?" I said, laughing, "I just had a couple of other ladies tell me how lovely and radiant I looked today! I think I like their appraisal better!" And then I hugged her. I refuse to allow other people's pessimism to affect me, no matter how well-intentioned they may be.

Viktor Frankl, concentration camp survivor and one of my favorite authors, wrote a book, *Man's Search for Meaning*. He said it was in the concentration camp experiences that he learned, "Everything can be taken from a man but one thing: the last of the human freedoms—to choose one's attitude in any given set of circumstances, to choose one's own way."

Our attitude is the most important characteristic of the quality of our life, as we deal with various aspects of aging. There will often be circumstances we can't change or control, but our attitude determines how we define our existence.

I've often said, *"It doesn't matter so much what happens to us as much as our attitude about what happens to us."* Will we let events beyond our control overwhelm us or will we choose to walk through our days with grace and dignity?

Decisions, decisions. To age gracefully with humor and a good attitude or not, that's the dilemma. It takes a long time to grow young. Part of growing young requires choosing to live joyfully in the midst of trials or difficult circumstances. In some cases it's necessary to, "Choose to be happy!"

POINTS TO PONDER

❖ "You are as young as your faith...as young as your self-confidence...as young as your hope...."

❖ Spontaneity keeps you young.

❖ You're never too old to have a second childhood!

❖ Learning to grow young is your choice.

❖ Be thankful for what you have—no whining.

❖ Your attitude determines your existence.

❖ Growing young requires joyful living.

Chapter 3

CHOOSE TO BE HAPPY!

"Act the way you'd like to be and soon you'll be the way you act," said Dr. George W. Crane. (See www.world of quotes.com)

Norman Vincent Peale put it this way, "The happiness habit is developed by simply practicing happy thinking. Make a mental list of happy thoughts and pass them through your mind several times every day."

With regard to choosing happiness and living in joy in the midst of trials or difficult circumstances, I simply say, "Choose to be happy!" Through the years, I've learned that living in joy is my personal responsibility. It is not up to someone else to make me happy.

"Most folks are about as happy as they choose to be," was the axiom of President Abraham Lincoln.

If you choose to smile, even when you don't feel like it, others will almost always respond automatically with a smile in return. A friend of mine said, "Smiling is rather like a kiss—in order to get any good out of it, you have to give it to someone else." However, that isn't necessarily so. We can choose smile or even laugh when alone and lighten our own life.

Physically, a smile requires the use of approximately 36 muscles, but a frown uses 97 muscles. Also, a smile releases the muscles on your scalp, which in turn lets the blood flow more easily, which brings more oxygen to the brain, which results in a buoyancy in your personality. At the point of choosing to smile, you may not feel happier, but as you continue to smile, releasing the oxygen into the brain, you actually become happier.

To return to my simple statement, "Choose to be happy," there is proof that it is not hype from some motivational speaker, but a physical fact. If you don't believe it, test it out. Smile while you are reading this chapter, and see if you don't feel better by the time you read the last page.

The wisdom of King Solomon supports this finding as well: "*A merry heart does good, like medicine, But a broken spirit dries the bones*" (Prov. 17:22 NKJV).

When speaking at conferences, I try to intersperse my teaching points with some light-hearted material so people don't go to sleep. At a women's conference in Wisconsin, everyone had been in sessions all morning and then we had a big lunch. Every speaker hates to be assigned to the after-lunch session. Out of an audience of 350 ladies, I didn't see one smiling face that afternoon. In fact, I might as well have been speaking Chinese for all of the response I was receiving.

"Am I speaking Chinese or something?" I smiled and asked. "If you're happy and understand what I'm saying, notify your face!" Of course, everyone laughed, smiled at each other and I continued, thankfully with smiles of response from the audience.

You may be thinking, "That's fine for you, Samantha, but you have no idea what my life is like." It's true, I don't. But then, you don't know the tragedies I've had to face either. However, I've learned that life is easier if we keep our joy on the journey—no matter how difficult our circumstances.

Sometimes you may feel like you've been searching for joy and happiness but all you come up with are dust bunnies and broken crayons. You're not alone. We all go through times of stress when the world seems to be full of disappointments and broken dreams.

IT'S POSSIBLE

Can you imagine how Joseph, in the Bible, felt being sold into slavery by his own brothers and then being falsely accused by Potiphar's wife and ending up in prison? (See Genesis 30–50.) Prisons in those days didn't have hot showers and TV time.

But no matter what trials came his way, Joseph kept his attitude right, and the Lord blessed him with favor even in the difficult places. I'm sure Joseph had many dismal, discouraging nights in the prison, but he didn't let that keep him from making it to the palace. He eventually became ruler over Egypt and was able to save his father and brothers and the Israelite people from death.

Thomas Edison certainly had reasons to be discouraged. He had many personal problems in his life; and although we know him as the inventor of the light bulb, hundreds of his inventions didn't work. He had to scrap them and start over, ignoring the weeks and months he may have devoted to a project.

"No, I'm not discouraged," Mr. Edison said, "because every wrong attempt discarded is another step forward." If only we could be like Mr. Edison when discouragement hounds our heels. (*The Wise and Witty Quote Book*, Allen Klein published 2005, page 398.)

Sometimes it's not even broken dreams but just the daily grind of living that gets to us. It's the little bits of life that fret and worry us; we can dodge an elephant, but we can't dodge a gnat. Keeping my joy is easy when I have an absence of conflict. The lesson we must learn, though, is developing the ability to cope with the tough situation and still keep our joy.

One morning when I was in Seattle for a speaking engagement, I had one of those gnat experiences. I turned on my computer to work on my newspaper column while munching on my breakfast fruit. My laptop froze about half way through the start-up program.

It was especially disconcerting because I was facing a deadline and didn't have much time to work on my column before a friend was to pick me up for lunch at the Columbia Tower Club, the tallest building in Seattle. I was looking forward to seeing the skyscrapers of Seattle and the Puget

Sound, as well as enjoying some great conversation. The view from the Tower Club's lofty perch in the Seattle sky makes the famous Space Needle look like a LEGO™ toy built by my grandson, Ramsey.

I hurriedly pressed the Control/Alt tab along with the Delete key as well as the ESC key, and numerous other keys, all to no avail. Finally, I decided to call the local IBM number in Seattle to see if someone could talk me through my problem. After numerous button-pushing escapades, I finally reached a person who asked for all kinds of numbers. Fortunately, I was able to find them on the bottom of the laptop.

Eventually I was put through to a tech person—Rick who sounded a lot like Sam Elliott of "The Sacketts" TV series and other Westerns. But with time slipping away, I had to attend to my problem not his attractive Sam Elliott voice!

Typical of these computer gurus, he was able to talk me through a maze of button-pushing sequences that quickly solved my problem. I thanked Rick profusely, explaining that I was traveling and how frustrating it was when little things like this interrupts the day.

"Well, when you get frustrated with these 'dad-burned' machines," Rick replied, "a little prayer wouldn't hurt."

"Sometimes a lot of prayer works even better," I responded, "but I forgot!" We both laughed and I thanked him again, grateful to get back to my column.

That incident was like a lot of little irritations in our day that, nevertheless, seem to bring life to a screeching halt.

When frustrations come, it is hard to remember to examine our attitude and choose joy.

Sometimes we talk and talk about our predicament of being single and not having a special someone to take us to a movie or out to dinner. The more we talk about our dilemmas, the more they become ingrained in our minds. Many of us manufacture our own unhappiness by the words we speak and the thoughts we think. The next time you're tempted to ramble on about your frustrations, stop and choose to move on to a more positive conversation. Make a deliberate effort to smile and keep smiling until you feel your emotions lift.

Another joy stealer is getting disconcerted about things over which we have no control. We feel helpless, like we're trying to punch our way out of a paper bag and we can't break out.

While I was working on this chapter, a friend, Bonnie, who lives in a country club community here in the desert, called me. She had been away for a few days, and the association management, at the request of her new neighbors, had removed a beautiful, old tree that was on common ground, but right in front of her patio. Bonnie loved that tree and had watched it grow from the time it was a small seedling. It provided welcomed shade for her patio as well as a home for many little singing birds.

"How could they do this to that lovely tree?" Bonnie said. Yes, she had put her house on the market to sell, but they still should have consulted her.

I let her vent and then I said, "Bonnie, remember the Serenity Prayer? It says to accept those things you cannot change. Well, the tree is already gone."

Even though Bonnie began to protest, I continued. "It's not going to make any difference to someone buying your house. They won't miss the tree, they have never seen it, and you can't stick it back in the ground. The tree is gone. Give it up."

"But it's not right," again Bonnie protested.

"You can't change it; accept it. Yes, your new neighbors should have consulted you, but they didn't. Let it go."

After much discussion, Bonnie was finally able to see the wisdom of letting go of her anger. It's so easy for anyone of us to get sidetracked. Letting it go didn't mean that removing the tree without consulting Bonnie was right. It wasn't. But by letting it go, Bonnie's blood pressure returned to normal and the ensuing headache went away.

Why agonize about problems we can't control? Let's get busy controlling what we can and what depends on us. An interesting change takes place as we change the word "problem" to challenge. Challenge denotes something we can work on, something that may take effort but can be changed.

Sometimes it may not be a specific, traceable event that steals our joy. Like all of us, Bonnie had to learn that a happy person is not a person in a certain set of circumstances but rather a person with a certain set of *attitudes*. This may be one of the most important principles we can learn as a Savvy Single.

Sometimes our days are filled with work pressures, family obligations, and responsibilities. We start to feel as if it will take every minute of the day just to get by. Who has time for joy?

There are people who seem to instinctively know how to find joy in the small serendipities of life. Most of us have to work at it. We have to learn to make a choice to be cheerful and look for joy.

24 HOURS IN EVERY DAY

Start looking for joy wherever you are. Being open to conversations with people I casually meet often brings laughter and joy at unexpected moments. Such was one of my conversations with Ginger Rogers.

Living in the Palm Springs area of California, I never know who will cross my path on a daily basis. For instance, in her later years, Ginger Rogers often had her nails manicured at the salon I went to, and she sat in the chair next to mine. She loved telling stories of her past career in the movies and regaling us with stories about dancing with Fred Astaire.

One day I mentioned a statement I had read in a magazine that was attributed to her. The article stated, "Ginger Rogers said, 'I did everything Fred Astaire did, but had to do it backward and in high heels.'" At that, she laughed a rich, deep belly laugh admitting it was true, she did say that. I smile even now when I think of the rich sound of her laughter.

Sometimes our day seems so full of pressures that we don't take time for joy. That may seem like a rather odd statement, but sometimes we must do exactly that—Take time for joy!

As you look at the past days, weeks, or months of your life, how often have you taken time to do something you really like to do? Something that gives you joy.

Let's look at how we spend our days. Sleep takes up 7-8 hours in the 24. If we work or volunteer time with an organization, that might take up another 8 hours. Eating maybe an hour total; cleaning up the kitchen and bath another hour. We've now used up 18 of the 24 hours in a day. That still gives us 5 full hours to choose what we want to do.

How many times do we complain that we don't have time to pursue a new career or a new hobby? Perhaps we really do. It's just a question of how we use those 5 free hours. Do we spend it in front of the TV "vegging out," wasting our brainpower and shutting down our creative juices? Too much idle, wasted time, steals our joy. In the hours left after TV, we feel overwhelmed, so we push creative pursuits or relaxing activities to the bottom of our daily list, thinking they are less important. Actually, it's in the pursuit of even the smallest of personal desires or creative dreams that our sense of well-being, our joy will return.

If you had 5 hours to spend any way you wanted, what would you choose to do with that time? What simple pleasures or pastimes bring you joy? Are you making time for them? Why not? As you think about these questions, write out the answers, you could even write them in the margins of this book. Then begin making time in your day for at least one item on your list. Make a decision to put joy and purpose into your life one step at a time.

As you read the chapters, let the principles and ideas awaken your long buried dreams. Begin to utilize more of these 5 hours for what you really want to do, not what is necessarily expected of you. It may be as simple as walking your dog in the early morning fog or spending more time with your grandchildren that will bring joy.

Looking for joy one day while I was in Montana, I invited two of my grandchildren up to the second floor balcony at my place on the lake.

Little Katie, who loves to talk, and her older brother, Ramsey, who at the time was a very pragmatic 6 year old, were very excited when I told them we were going to have a special "sunflower seed-spitting contest." And so we did. The shells, spit over the balcony with the late afternoon sun shining on them, looked a lot like angel dust as they floated down to the grass below. Well, as least we thought so.

Events like these are good times for giggling and talking about everything that is really important, such as the deer passing near the fence or laughing at the new puppy's antics or the Bible stories they are learning.

Ramsey brought up a new story he had learned about Moses floating down the river in a little basket. Katie kept interrupting, as she hadn't heard the story before. It was amusing when pragmatic Ramsey stopped our conversation and explained to Katie the reason she didn't know yet about Moses floating in his little basket on the river was because she wasn't in first grade yet.

Watching their little animated faces, I was reminded of a study done at the University of Michigan by Dr. Zajone, proposing the theory that as certain facial muscles relax or tighten, they raise or lower the temperature of blood flowing to the brain. These changes in temperature, in turn affect the activity brain centers that regulate emotion.

In Dr. Zajone's opinion, simply smiling or laughing may relieve a headache if the cause of it is stress related whereby the muscles in the scalp have tightened. As we smile or laugh, he says, it releases those muscles, allowing more blood flow to the brain.

Medically, doctors know that good blood flow to the brain is critical for efficient and comprehensive brain functioning. So when we laugh more, it stands to reason we should have a better functioning brain. Maybe that's the reason I keep forgetting where I put my glasses, I'm not laughing enough!

If we are going through a stress-filled day, and make the decision to have even one moment in the day for ourselves, to experience laughter and joy, it will change our lives. We must train ourselves to keep looking at the possibilities in any situation rather than the problems. We will amaze ourselves as solutions appear and we handle the challenge more effectively.

My friend, Margie, from Dallas, Texas recently shared a story about a stressful day at her office. A set of important loan documents went missing that morning and considerable time was spent trying to solve their mysterious disappearance. She was silently blaming herself for what must have been a "senior moment" memory lapse.

In the middle of the afternoon, her boss walked in the door with the papers confessing he had found them in the back seat of his Hummer. Quickly Margie arranged for a courier to make a one-hour delivery to the bank. The envelope was left at the reception desk for the courier to pick up.

At 5 P.M. Margie's boss called saying that the bank had received a very strange package containing Dallas Cowboys sprinkler heads but no loan papers! She immediately went to the reception desk and to her horror found her envelope still there.

The company owns newsstands and sells numerous retail items but Margie could not imagine how Dallas Cowboys sprinkler heads fit in the picture or how the courier got that box. The more she thought about her day and about how ridiculous this incident was the more she giggled.

When she called the company's buyer and found out that the buyer had been frantically looking for the box of sprinkler heads, Margie laughed until she cried. It was a comedy of errors how the courier ended up at the loading dock instead of the reception desk and picked up the box of sprinklers by mistake, but the stress of the day was completely dispelled by laughter. Margie said she could have had a tension headache but instead she giggled out loud all the way home. And yes, fans at the Dallas/Fort Worth International Airport will buy anything that says Dallas Cowboys on it!

But if you're having one of those horrendous days when everything continues to go wrong, try smiling anyway and when the muscles in your face start to relax, you will find your spirits lifting. Eventually, you will feel better even if your circumstances haven't changed. As I said before, "Choose to be happy!" It's your ticket to a more contented life.

Sometimes we're run so ragged by life that we don't even know what we want anymore. Desires and creative urges get lost as we simply try to keep up with our horrendous schedule of busyness.

Let's take a few minutes and try a simple exercise that can stretch your imagination and help you develop new outlets for creativity and leisure. Remember, the best time to relax is when you're too busy to relax. Do not feel guilty when you take a few moments to relax, to dream. I challenge you to try it.

1. Sit or lie comfortably and take several slow, deep breaths.

2. As best you can, clear your mind of intrusive thoughts. Take a few minutes and if any negative thoughts flow through your mind, acknowledge them and then let them go as you exhale.

3. Picture yourself three months from now. Ask yourself, "In an ideal world, how would I spend my free time?" Focus on an image of yourself in any setting or activity that brings you joy. You may be surprised as a long-forgotten dream or desire begins to surface.

4. Now that you know what that dream or desire is, you have the choice to implement it in your life now.

Lately I haven't taken much time for myself, so I stopped and practiced this simple activity. In the process of developing my goals and dreams, I hadn't stopped to consider what would bring me joy, right now.

As I sat, closed my eyes and exhaled, I quickly realized what I wanted to incorporate back into my life to bring joy. I would like to get back to playing golf, something I hadn't done on a regular basis since my husband, Morry, died. Now that I know what latent desire had been lurking in my mind, I can decide whether I want to implement it.

I hope this revealing exercise opens up new creative desires and ideas for you too. It may be as simple as taking time to read a new book or spending more time with your grandchildren or it may be learning a new skill.

Remember to take time for joy, remember to smile.

POINTS TO PONDER

❖ "The happiness habit is developed by simply practicing happy thinking...." Dr. Norman Vincent Peale

❖ Smiling is like kissing—share it with someone else.

❖ Life is easier if you are joyful.

❖ Learn to dodge the elephants *and* the gnats.

❖ Manufacture your own happiness.

❖ A happy person chooses the right attitude.

❖ In the pursuit of even the smallest personal desire or creative dream your joy will return.

❖ The best time to relax is when you're too busy to relax.

Chapter 4

SCRUB OUT YOUR INSIDES WITH LAUGHTER

I've included many quotations and jokes in this chapter to prove my point that each one of us can choose to be happy—especially by laughing. Most of the authors of the quotes and quips are identified, but some were sent to me by e-mail with no author cited—any slight is unintentional.

The exquisite dinner was finished and we sat in the elegant restaurant, finishing our coffee. It was very romantic looking out the window at the city below turning golden in the sunset. I turned to my dinner date and thanked him for bringing me to one of my favorite restaurants in the whole world. Ambiance has always been a huge part of whether or not I like a restaurant.

"Don't you sometimes have a yen to kiss and giggle?" he said, smiling as his eyes became very mischievous.

Knowing my dinner date was suggesting something beyond "kiss and giggle," I wanted to answer carefully without hurting his feelings, yet I wanted to make it very clear that, if so, he had chosen the wrong person to invite out for the evening. Turning to look out the window while quickly forming my answer, I guess I was mumbling the words for the response to myself.

"Samantha, you'll have to speak a little louder when you're talking about sex!" My date said loudly and I could feel a blush forming on my cheeks. Suddenly I burst out laughing.

Some of the people at the adjoining tables must have heard him as laughter joined in from all around the room. It was a memorable night of fun, albeit without any "kiss and giggle." Laughter did indeed scrub out my insides, making me feel young again. However, in the remaining moments of that evening, I gave thanks in my heart for the maturity of being a Savvy Single able to say "no" to any possibility of what "kiss and giggle" might lead to.

But returning to the point of God's wonderful gift of laughter, and its ability to scrub out our insides during times of difficulty, it truly is a gift that can play a huge part in keeping us young. Many couples that have been married 50 years or more cite humor as one of the reasons they have remained happily married, saying how much it helped them get through the tough times they have faced.

I remember my dad often invited his rancher and cattle-buyer friends to stop by our house. They would drink coffee and tell stories. My dad loved telling funny stories from the pioneer days, often laughing so hard while he was telling the story that he could hardly finish it. My gramp was like that too. I believe that's one reason everyone in our little town and the farms around gravitated toward them and enjoyed being with them.

In our busy, over-committed world, laughter seems to have been lost along the way. We don't find much of it in our everyday lives. We seem to leave it up to the professional comedians to supply us with our daily dose of laughter.

One lady, Melody Fleming, a CLL (Certified Laugh Leader) started a business called, "Laffing Matters" in order to spread the word about the importance of humor for our health. Her goal is to offer tips and ideas on how to create more joy and laughter in everyday life. She believes "many of us are suffering from hardening of the attitudes, which can be fatal to having fun."

Years ago I started keeping a notebook of jokes and cartoons, some of them from *Reader's Digest* or other periodicals and sometimes just funny things that happened to me or to friends. When I get down or feel rather flat, I often to go my "Joy Box" and read stuff until I start to giggle and eventually laugh. It's good for my soul. Here are a few jokes from my Joy Box that I hope will make you laugh—after all, it's good for you!

This is an old Milton Berle joke from 1989.

An old woman is having a heck of a time with a parking place. A good Samaritan stops to tell her which way to turn. "This way, that way, more that way, this way." Finally the old woman's car is safely nestled between two others. The good Samaritan nods, but before he can leave, the old lady says, "Thank you, but I was trying to get out!"

This is just one of the many funny sayings that I love. It is credited to Groucho Marx.

"Outside of a dog, a book is man's best friend. Inside a dog, it's too dark to read."

Since this is a chapter about laughter, I hope you will practice laughing. Here's another joke I love.

A Sunday school teacher was teaching her class about the difference between right and wrong, specifically about not stealing.

"All right children, let's take another example." she said, "If I were to get into a man's pocket and take his billfold with all of his money, what would I be?"

Little Johnny raises his hand, and with a confident smile, he blurts out, "You'd be his wife!" (Probably more true than any of us would like to admit!)

I've been thinking a lot about laughter lately, and the power it has in our lives. Of course, my favorite is affirming, loving words from someone who thinks I'm terrific and makes me laugh! I had one such phone call today and after I hung up, I had a little smile in my heart all day.

What happens when we don't have someone to encourage us and life gets tough? I imagine most people are like I am; we have all had formidable issues in life, perhaps some more than others. But even during the difficult times, we can choose our attitude about life. We may not be able to change the circumstance, but we can choose how we respond to it.

Not too long ago I was traveling and had put in a long, 8-hour day on the road. I was really tired. The movie "Legally Blonde" was at the movie theatre in this little town. I noticed that it was rated PG13 and was supposed to be funny.

I have studied enough about affirming words and laughter to know that good, out-loud laughter actually releases endorphins in the brain. When endorphins are released into the body, oxygen is released into the brain and we feel uplifted and relaxed. So I went to the movie and indeed did laugh, often!

It's been said that laughter is like scrubbing out our insides and I felt that way after the movie. Outside, the tragic circumstances in my life had not changed, but inside my body, I had changed. I was more relaxed and able to face my life, which was very painful at that particular time.

Recently I heard someone say laughter is her "drug of choice." Hmm. Since endorphins are known in science to be stronger than morphine, I guess laughter is a pretty good "drug" for all of us to choose.

During this same time of my life, knowing I needed to laugh, an author friend of mine sent me a book, *She Who Laughs Last!*, Compiled by Ann Spangler. It's a compilation of funny stories written by different authors. It has intriguing chapter titles like, "A Laugh a Day Puts Wrinkles in the Right Places." Reading it did put some wrinkles in the right places in spite of my circumstances.

I think often of my Aunt Bertha who lived until she was over 102. The thing I remember most about her, besides the single strand of pearls she always wore, was the fact she laughed about everything!

When she was in her late 80s and living in Minnesota, I called her one winter day when it was 24 below zero and snowing. She laughed while telling me about falling in the snow that morning while shoveling the sidewalk.

Her biggest concern was not that she might get hurt but as she was struggling to get up out of the snow bank, she suddenly thought how ridiculous she would look if she got stuck there and in the spring when the snow thawed, the first thing they would see was her funny red cap she was wearing. She laughed again as she told me that just thinking about them finding her red cap on the top of her head, spurred her on with energy to get out of the snow bank!

Being born in the late 1800s, life for Aunt Bertha in the Dakotas and Minnesota certainly wasn't easy; but no matter what tragedy or difficulty was in her life, she faced it with courage and lots of laughter! From the time I was a little girl, I wanted to be a lady like Aunt Bertha.

Years later, as an adult, I wrote to her when my husband gave me my first strand of pearls to tell her I was on my way to becoming a lady like she was. Now that I had pearls, I just needed to learn to laugh more. Well, as you can imagine, when she received the letter and called me, we laughed a lot about that!

In my study of laughter, I read that doctors are examining the positive power of laughter on our body. However,

King Solomon wrote about it 4,000 years ago in Proverbs, *"A merry heart does good like a medicine."* I'm glad doctors are finally finding out what God knew all along!

So, if life is tough or simply boring, read a funny book or go to a comedy movie and laugh. It's better than medicine and much more fun!

Last year my friend Gwen and her husband Patrick invited me to attend a Bill Cosby performance. I have always loved his routines—I can still remember his deep voice dialogue between God and Abraham as Abraham found out about circumcision.

Since I always have a hard time finding my glasses, one of the more memorable things Cosby said that night at his show was, "I wear glasses, primarily so I can look for the things I keep losing, like my glasses!"

As I have been working on laughing more, I discovered I tend to be more like the stand-up comedian who makes everyone else laugh. However, that doesn't scrub the inside of my body so I'm concentrating on laughing more too.

Some say laughter is the language of the young at heart and the antidote to what ails us. Laughter's benefits show on our face, in our body language, and in the spring in our step. I've heard it said that laughing heartily has the same beneficial effects as daily exercise. Did you know one good laugh burns and estimated six calories?

Perhaps if we want to get to know someone, we should forget about analyzing what she says and watch to see how much she laughs. If I were an employer, I'd hire the person who laughs well. As a single woman, one of the qualities I watch for in a man is one who laughs easily. If I were looking for a special friend, I'd search until I met a woman who laughs well. Maybe I need to be sure I'm that kind of friend too.

Interestingly, we are the only creatures created to giggle and laugh. Maybe there is one exception, the laughing hyena. Although it sounds as if he is laughing, in reality, that's the way he barks, the way he communicates.

We have the capacity to be tickled way deep down inside. Giggles are as contagious as a viral disease. I've noticed that when my grandchildren giggle, so do I. We laugh about their somersaults that end up sideways. We laugh about their drawing of me with my little round glasses on, holding a big flower, larger than me!

When the losses in life become unbearable, we'll handle them better if we remember to keep our sense humor. Oh, there may be nothing funny in the circumstance that has us in its grip, but we can choose to laugh at the antics of our neighbor's new cat or read funny jokes, or watch children play.

In the book, *A View from the Pew*, from Guidepost, Martin Luther is credited with saying, "If you're not allowed to laugh in Heaven, I don't want to go there." Since laughter is God's idea, he won't have to worry about that.

SMILE SIGHTINGS

A few years ago I decided to practice what I write about while I was walking around in the Salt Lake City airport late on New Year's Eve. It's not the most exhilarating place I could imagine, but there I was with a 2 $1/2$-hour layover on my way home to Palm Springs. After I ordered my cup of White Chocolate Cappuccino at Starbucks and sat down to enjoy it, I noticed immediately that no one was smiling. I mean no one. It was obvious that they didn't want to be there on New Year's Eve either.

Since I didn't have a good book to read and wasn't in the mood to work on the computer, I decided to exercise. So I put a bounce in my step and began walking up and down the long terminal walkways making eye contact with as many people as possible and smiling, really big!

It was fun. There seemed to be three classes of people. The first group, thankfully a small group, actually scowled at me, thinking I had no right to smile at them. They were unhappy and that was the way they were going to stay. They seemed to say, "Get out of the way and leave me alone in my mood."

The second group returned the smile and some people in this group even said hello, thinking they must know me, otherwise why would I be smiling. However, they hurried past so they wouldn't be embarrassed if indeed I stopped to talk to them and they couldn't recall who I was.

The third group smiled widely in return like we shared some secret—which we did. We were choosing to smile in spite of being in no man's land on New Year's Eve.

Finally, it was time to get on the plane. This was a small carrier and so we had to walk out on the tarmac to the plane. As we stood waiting at the hallway door, three young women starting complaining because it was snowing outside and they were going to get snow in their hair. So I turned to this lovely white-haired lady and her husband beside me and said, "Oh, isn't it simply wonderful to see the snow coming down so softly. What better gift could we have on New Year's Eve?"

As our conversation continued, I mentioned the snowflakes looked pink in the arc of the tarmac lights. Soon others joined in our conversation and slowly the mood changed as we waited to get on the plane, each of us anticipating the joy of walking through the softly falling snow on this New Year's Eve of 2001. The large, lazy snowflakes were just magnificent.

Once again, I'd proven to myself that we really can affect our world by our attitude. In my own little way, I brought joy and friendliness to a group of strangers who had nothing in common except they happened to be at the same place at the same time. The conversations even continued on the plane since we were such a small group, it was almost like family as people chatted back and forth.

Now I'm not naïve enough to believe that simply smiling at people will change their world. No, I still had the same problems I had before I got on the plane. I was still not excited about coming home to Palm Springs to face the New Year alone. But one thing smiling at people did for me, was to help me relax and be thankful for what I do have. I may not have had someone to kiss as the New Year came in, but there's always next year!

When life is difficult, it's time to laugh. One of my favorite sayings is: *Life is not for sissies. It takes tenacity to put laughter and joy into our lives.* So these days I am seeking out events that make me laugh and, "scrub out my insides with laughter."

Scrub Out Your Insides With Laughter

There was one night in particular when I knew I could find laughter. Harvey Korman, Tim Conway, and Louise DuArt came to the McCallum Theatre with their comedy show. Although Louise told me backstage they have been doing the show in theatres all over the United States for five years, it was as fresh and funny as though it was the first time they had performed it.

Harvey and Tim, of course, have had years working on their timing on the "Carol Burnett" TV show as well as numerous other venues. It was fun to watch them ad-lib from their routine and make each other laugh.

Thankfully, I was sitting with a couple of friends who are good at laughing out loud, too. So my howls of laughter, with mascara streaming down my cheeks, didn't seem out of place. Even the nice, quiet little man on my left finally laughed. It might have been in self-defense since we three were having such a great time, along with the rest of the audience.

Between the Harvey and Tim rip-roaring routines, Louise did impersonations. The transition between the three was smooth and wonderful as they introduced each other, with Harvey introducing Louise as "George Burns and Gracie Allen."

Dressed in a black tuxedo, "he" shuffled on stage, wearing his big thick glasses and smoking his unlit cigar. As he began his routine in his gravelly voice, it seemed as if George Burns was actually speaking. With impeccable timing, he said, "You know I'm almost 100 now and when I was a kid, the Dead Sea was only sick!"

Following George's routine was the usual Gracie and George banter—except Louise was doing it. With the simple removal of "his" glasses, she was able to totally change her face and her voice in that split second timing she does so well, becoming each character.

Louise DuArt has been performing impersonations on stage for 23 years (she must have started when she was 6!). I lost count how many people "come on stage" with her. Her Barbara Walters was hilarious. Cher singing and swinging her long black hair along with the line, "I change my wigs more than I do my underwear," made one wonder if Cher herself was this good. And her Katherine Hepburn was sensational. Louise sounded just like we remember Katherine with her shaky, New England accent.

Finally, the curtain falls on a spectacular, funny show. As the audience finally stopped applauding, the majority stood in small groups all over the auditorium talking and laughing and retelling the refreshingly clean jokes.

Back stage you would have thought the three performers were still on stage. As we greeted them, their responses were as funny as their routines. Some comedians are only funny at delivering their lines, but these three are delightfully funny people who are a joy to be around. While Louise is extraordinarily funny, she told me it is her relationship with Christ that enables her to radiate her joy from within.

In the book, *"You've Gotta Be Kidding"* from Guideposts, J.John and Mark Stiffe have written the following joke.

The Japanese eat little fat and suffer fewer heart attacks than the British or Americans.

The French eat a lot of fat and also suffer fewer heart attacks than the British or Americans.

The Italians drink a lot of red wine and they, too, suffer fewer heart attacks than the British or Americans.

Conclusion: Eat and drink what you like. Speaking English is apparently what kills you!

I found the following joke in my minister's newsletter. I hope it makes you smile too.

Mrs. Willencot was very frugal. When her husband died, she asked the newspaper how much it would cost for a death notice.

"Two dollars for five words."

"Can I pay for just two words?"

"No, five words is the minimum."

Mrs. Willencot thought for a moment, "OK, then. How about this? 'Willencot dead. Cadillac for sale.'"

This is just a sampling of the jokes and funny sayings I have collected in my Joy Box through the years. I also keep amusing letters from friends, cute drawings from my grandchildren, and anything else that makes me smile.

Then when life gets tough, or I am feeling particularly lonely, I can go to my Joy Box and sift through the well-worn contents. Even such simple statements as one by Phyllis Diller, brings a smile to my face and I am ready to go on. She said, "They say that housework won't kill you, but why take the chance!"

"My best friend ran away with my wife," Henry Young-man said, "And let me tell you, I really miss him."

One of my pleasures in life is to have friends who can remember jokes. Dorree, my secretary, is good at remembering jokes and my friend Geri loves to tell jokes. This is her latest, and maybe best, offering. I think she got it on an e-mail.

Mabel's husband, George, was really ill. In fact, the doctor had informed them that George was indeed going to die. As Mabel is sitting by George's bed, she notices he is deep in thought. Seeking to console him, she asks George what he is thinking about.

"Well," George says, with a far away look in his eyes, "I've been thinking about when I'm gone and I want you to marry so you won't be lonely."

"Oh, no," Mabel hastily replied, "We've had a wonderful marriage and I don't want to even think about anyone else."

"But it will give me peace, just knowing you won't be alone."

Finally, Mabel was convinced George was serious so she reluctantly agreed she would be open to a new husband.

George lies there in serious thought and then looks at Mabel, "When you do get married again, does that mean he will sleep in my bed?"

"Yes, George," Mabel gently replies, "That's what married people do, they sleep together, so we would be sleeping in our bed."

Again George thinks awhile. "Does that mean he will be driving my truck?"

"Well, it is all paid for and we would need transportation," Mabel hesitantly says.

This time there is a long silence and George whispers, "Will he be using my golf clubs too?"

"No, George, he's left-handed." (Smile!)

So, dear Savvy Single friend, go out and start filling up your own Joy Box, let the joy inside you help you through your arduous, perplexing and often complicated life. Scrub out your insides with laughter, today and every day. Remember, each belly laugh burns six calories!

Laughter provides a powerful emotional release from the stress every Savvy Single endures from time to time. It can also help to dispel another emotional force that we all face— fear. Let's explore how to make sure you know how to win as a "Fear Factor" contestant.

POINTS TO PONDER

❖ God's wonderful gift of laughter will keep you young.

❖ Even during the difficult times, choose your attitude about life.

❖ Laughter is the language of the young at heart and the antidote to what ails you.

❖ Giggles are as contagious as a viral disease.

❖ Life is not for sissies.

Chapter 5

ARE YOU A "FEAR FACTOR" CONTESTANT?

Have you ever thought about what it would be like to be a contestant on the TV show, "Fear Factor?" I would wager a guess that most Savvy Singles would say, "No way! I would never do anything like that." I'll admit that eating worms or being dumped into a snake pit is not my idea of entertainment. This popular "reality" show borders on the grotesque at times, but one thing I can say about the contestants is that for whatever reason or motive, they courageously face their fears head on. We could all learn a lesson from such courage because in reality we are all contestants in the "fear factor" of every day life.

Of necessity, I was scheduled to fly a few days after 9-11-2001. Of course, all flights in the U.S. were grounded and so I waited on pins and needles glued to the news channel.

When the planes were released to fly about seven days later, I was only one of about 20 people on a plane that could hold over 300. As I walked the runway to the plane, I looked back at my loved ones, wondering if I would ever see them again. Yes, I had a lot of fear, but I chose not to let it dominate me. *Courage is not the absence of fear; it is the conquest of it!*

Fear is one of the most powerful forces we encounter in life. There are times our fear is justified, other times it isn't. But for most of us, we've learned to mask our fear well. We've learned to smile, give the firm handshake, that air of assurance that says we have it all together—but inside we're trembling and afraid.

Fear takes on many forms. The list is endless and individual. Some people are afraid of dogs, snakes, bats, or mice. Others are afraid of being on a boat, snow skiing, or being in tall buildings. You can continue the list with your own fears. But perhaps the most pervasive fear we all deal with at various times of our lives is the fear of failure.

I remember my grandma, sitting on her front porch, telling me I could accomplish anything I wanted to with my life. However, we never discussed how to overcome all the fear factors, such as possible failures, that I would face on my journey to success.

Even at an early age, I wanted to teach and write books. My earliest "book" was one my mother kept for me. I found it in my box of memories that Mom had sorted for each one of us children in her later years. In my box were old report cards, pictures, Sunday school awards and even old letters I had written to her. Near the bottom of the box was a little six-page book, tied together with a pink bow. The title was

"To my mother." It told in child-like phrases of why I loved my mom. The last page said, simply, "My mother smiles when she tucks me in bed. I love you, Mom."

In high school, at the urging of a teacher, I submitted a poem to a literary magazine, and they liked it enough to publish it. I was hooked. Then, somewhere along the way, I got sidetracked and put my literary dreams aside for other dreams—often, other people's dreams.

It was many years later when I finally had the courage to start writing again for publication. But the fear of rejection almost overwhelmed me. I hated getting rejection letters from publishers. I had to learn that the rejection letter was not a personal affront to me, nor did it say I had failed. It helped me to say to myself, "Well, it's their loss," and send my article out to another publisher.

I love how motivational speaker, Zig Ziglar, describes failure. He says, "Failure is an event, not a person." When we take failure personally, it can devastate us, but when we view it as an event, we can turn it from a negative to a positive change factor.

No one likes to fail. Failure is especially difficult if it was something in which you really believed and had put in a lot of effort. Whether it is failed relationships or failed dreams, it's devastating.

"I have not failed. I've just found 10,000 ways that won't work," is an interesting quote by Thomas Edison. It's a great to have an attitude like that about failure.

If we learn to rise up, after falling flat on our face, and begin again, failure often turns into something better. But it's the pits when you're going through it.

It took me years to realize that I had a hard time accepting failure because I was never taught how to fail. Are we ever? The world loves winners. Our culture celebrates winners. Everyone wants to be around champions whether it is the Super Bowl, the Olympics, or the Masters of the golfing world.

The publishing industry offers a proliferation of books teaching us how to be winners. I have bought them, read them, and applied them. But sometimes, no matter how much we want something, how hard we work at something; we fail. Fear of failure is a subtle pervasive fear factor that settles deep in the pit of our stomachs.

Sometimes a relationship fails, no matter how hard we try. Sometimes a dream job we want doesn't materialize. Sometimes things we want to do, don't work out. A house we want to buy is sold before we can make an offer. We may lose a job.

A spouse or a loved one may have failures, which affect us too. It took me years to realize that I can only be responsible for me. I can't fix other people's failures or shortcomings. When we finally let other people work out their own problems and work on our own issues, life is easier.

My friend, Wanda, called not long ago, all upset because of the issues surrounding her stepchildren. Even though they are now grown and live in other cities, when birthdays, weddings, and other events happen, there is always some kind of conflict. Her health has often been affected by the frustration and anger, wanting to protect her husband from his controlling, manipulating children from a previous marriage.

Somehow I could not get through to her that she will only fail if she tries to fix things. The issue is not who is right or wrong, what matters is realizing we can't change other people or the choices they make. The best thing we can do is to pray for them and let God take care of the rest.

While I may not like it, in my life I have learned that failure often turns out to be a "good thing." If we choose to learn from failure, it can provide building blocks for our soul. Through adversity, our will and emotions can become healed and strengthened.

Think of the successful people we have heard of, who failed many, many times before they succeeded. Examples include:

❖ R.H. Macy failed seven times in business before his successful New York store.

❖ English novelist John Creasey accumulated 733 rejection slips before he went on to publish 564 books.

❖ Hal Lindsay had 37 publishers reject *The Late Great Planet Earth* before he found one who would take it.

❖ Babe Ruth struck out 1,330 times but he also hit 714 home runs.

❖ Thomas Edison was actually trying to invent something else when he stumbled onto the light bulb. He had thousands of experiments that never worked, but failure didn't stop him.

I *THINK* I CAN

The point is that success and failure come in the same package. When someone is successful, we don't mean she never makes mistakes; we mean that her successes outweigh her failures. *No one is a complete success or a complete failure.*

You may *feel* like a failure but that's the catch, because feelings dominate self-perception and affect performance. If we allow feelings to dominate, then failure will breed failure, just like success will produce success.

I learned this in an easy lesson through golf. While I'm a pretty good golfer with a reasonably low handicap, I had always been pathetic getting out of sand traps. Because I knew I was horrible at it, I couldn't do it.

One day while playing with a man who is a 4 handicapper, I told him about my difficulties in getting out of traps. After our game, he gave me some lessons on shooting out of a sand trap and had me practice until I was doing it consistently.

"Now you know how to do it, Samantha," he instructed, "You must tell yourself you can do it, each time you need to chip out of the trap."

And so that is what I do. When someone says, "Oh you poor dear, you're in the trap." I reply, "That's okay, I'm good at getting out of sand traps." And so I do!

Even though I had some skills before the lesson, the main difference is my attitude. Because I *think* I can do it, I can!

We need to learn to control our feelings, whether it is in something as simple as golf, or as complex as relationships, business, or learning a new skill. Failure in itself is insignificant. It's what we do afterward that counts.

Accept failure as your identity, and you will fail the rest of your life. View it as an opportunity to change, and it can be the door to great success.

At a very young age, Tom Harken had polio and spent a long time in an iron lung. Then even after he was home, he was quarantined to his room because they thought he also had Tuberculosis. So he missed a lot of school. When he finally returned to school he was a "very big kid at a very little desk." People made fun of him because he could not read or write and so, even though he was still a child, he quit school.

While selling vacuum cleaners door-to-door and many other jobs, Tom suffered greatly because he could not read. One day his wife, Melba, decided she would do something to help him. Little by little, as Tom worked with Melba at their kitchen table after the children were in bed, she taught him to read. His early failures became past history as Tom began to experience success in various business ventures. Eventually, he started what would become the multi-million dollar business, Casa Ole' restaurant chain.

When Tom became the recipient of the Horatio Alger Award in 1992, he knew he had to share his secret about not being able to read for so many years. This award gave him the platform to be able to help others and inspire them to overcome their own difficulties.

Tom is now an advocate for literacy working with Barbara Bush. His enthusiasm for life makes him someone we all want to be around. He inspires others to be the best they can be and dream big dreams, because God has a plan for their lives.

No matter what the pattern has been in our past, failure at any level doesn't have to be forever. But if we're going to change, we have to adopt what salespeople call a "winning attitude." Failure is only terminal if we allow it to be; otherwise it can become a useful form of education.

On one "Fear Factor" episode, several beautiful young women were competing against the clock in an event that required walking a tightrope stretched between two buildings several stories above a busy street. They were secured in a harness and had ropes extended for them to hold onto as they made the perilous journey across the rope. But even with all that protection the thought of falling at such a height and swinging through the air was daunting.

The contestants were cheering each other on and shouting words of encouragement from the street below. When the last contestant prepared to take her walk, the mood suddenly changed in the group of contestants. For some reason, the others did not like this last woman, and they started taunting her with words of discouragement. As they shouted, "You can't do it; you're going to fall; you won't make it across," the young woman became visibly shaken. About half way across the tightrope, she lost her balance and fell.

She was the only one out of the group who fell. It wasn't that she was any less skilled or capable of making the walk. In fact, she was more athletic than many of the other contestants and seemed very sure of herself as she put on the harness. However, her attitude was effected by the negative words being shouted at her as she stepped out onto the rope. Fear of failure crept in as she listened to the ugly words from her co-horts. She lost her confidence and then lost her footing.

How often do we lose our footing because of discouraging words spoken by others around us that destroy our winning attitude? We must guard ourselves from listening to negative words and from the impact of negative attitudes of those around us.

We need to learn from the failures of our past, *but* it is a major error to go into tomorrow, lugging the weight of our past mistakes with us.

We fail at all kinds of things, large and small. I've failed at diets. I've failed at keeping up an exercise program. I've failed in relationships, sometimes not being there when someone needed me. I've been hurt by people I loved—people who I had poured my heart into but was rejected.

Dealing with failure was hard in the past and it's still hard. No matter how many books we read on self-esteem and how to cope, we're still frail and fragile in our emotions, vulnerable to others.

OVERCOMING FEAR

But it's in dealing with my failures, that I've learned how to cope with it in a healthier manner. Cheryl Salem, Miss America 1980, said, "I give myself about 10 minutes to cry and commiserate and then I choose to get out of that. I choose to be happy." That has been a good learning tool for me. I don't always manage to keep my pity party to only 10 minutes, but I did learn that we must choose to get ourselves out of our emotional trauma.

If we choose to overcome the fear factor of failure, it will help us look at what we could have done differently. Was it really the path we wanted or is there something better out there to strive to attain? Sometimes I've found when I let something go that just isn't working out, something better comes along that is even more fulfilling. It's in letting it go that we will find the peace and time to evaluate what we should do next.

Fear of failure is not the only fear, even though it can impede us at every level. There is the fear of living alone. Some of us have been thrust into that situation without any choice. In today's crime-ridden culture, we do need to take precautions and use wisdom.

Simple things like being observant of our surroundings and other people when we are walking to our car, looking over our shoulder to be certain we are safe, are necessities. Watching to be sure we are not being followed in our car makes good sense. If you find yourself in a dangerous situation or your instinct makes you uneasy, retreat and get back to safety. A Savvy Single knows that retreating or running from danger is always the best solution. Police recommend that if you are approached by a carjacker and told to get into your car, drop whatever you are carrying or throw it at the person and run away. He is more likely to just take your car than try to chase you down. Cars can be replaced—people cannot.

But it's important as we adjust to living alone that we not allow our imagination to bring us into fear. For instance, I lock my doors when I go out to protect my possessions. Then I lock my doors when I am at home to protect my life. It's just good sense. How we choose to conquer our fear factors will make all the difference in the new life we create for ourselves as Savvy Singles.

I have friends my age who will not drive on the busy freeways. We get very lazy here in the California desert. We don't have to drive the multilane highways for anything we want to do, which is necessary in the Los Angeles area. Yet, if we wish to go to the beach or visit friends in that area, drive the freeway we must. It is stressful. It's not my most favorite thing to do, but I'm not going to let fear keep me from living my life to the fullest extent.

There are many challenges to learning to live alone. We are going to look at some very practical things in the following chapters. By choosing to face and overcome the very basic emotion of fear, you will be a successful fear factor contestant on your journey through life as a Savvy Single.

POINTS TO PONDER

- ❖ Courage is the conquest of fear!

- ❖ "Failure is an event, not a person." Zig Ziglar

- ❖ Learning from failure provides building blocks for your soul.

- ❖ Success and failure come in the same package.

- ❖ Accept failure as an opportunity door to great success.

- ❖ Failure is not terminal; it is an education.

- ❖ Learn from your failures but don't lug them into your future.

- ❖ A Savvy Single intelligently runs from danger.

- ❖ Conquering your fear factors creates new life.

SECTION TWO:

Dot Your I's and Cross Your T's

INTRODUCTION

Years ago, the saying, "Dot Your I's and Cross Your T's" was a familiar phrase. Basically, it meant be careful and thorough in all of your dealings and relationships. And that's what I will convey in this section of the book.

When we are newly single, for whatever reason, often we are too trusting. As women we are usually too trusting of people we consider an "authority" in some field of expertise. We may make decisions that will affect the rest of our lives without waiting, analyzing, and praying about it. The Bible also says we should seek counsel in Proverbs 11:14 (KJV), *"Where no counsel is, the people fall: but in the multitude of counselors there is safety."* So check your decisions with friends and associates who will give you wise and honest counsel.

People are also usually too trusting of the opposite gender when in the past they have had the buffer of a spouse to discuss the pros and cons of any given situation, whether it be financial, legal, or relational. When it comes to new friendships, it is wise to ask your close friends early on what they think about the person you have met. If they are truly a friend, they will tell you the truth. But I have found that most of the time they won't speak up unless you ask. So ask!

In this section we will explore some important legal and practical matters that every Savvy Single needs to consider. If you don't understand some legal terms or financial concepts, find an expert who will take the time to explain it to you. Do your own research. You can educate yourself in many areas by reading books that are available today on any subject. You can also search out reliable sources on the Internet if you're computer savvy. God bless each one of you on your journey to become a knowledgeable Savvy Single.

Chapter 6

WE ARE OUR BOUNDARIES

If you were watching TV, you would probably see a "viewer discretion" message flash across the screen right about now. I feel I have an obligation to write about some things that seniors try not to think about. Ignorance is not bliss when people's lives are at stake. Therefore, I am warning you that we are going to cover some sensitive material in this chapter. Some Christians may not think it's necessary; but we are living in the 21st century and this is no reality TV show—it's real life.

I was shocked! I couldn't believe my eyes. I even checked to be certain I was indeed reading the *USA Today* and not one of the sensational newspapers you buy at the grocery checkout stand.

But yes, I was reading the page 4 of the *USA Today* during the summer of 2003. The picture showed a nice looking, mature lady sitting at a desk. The article explained that she had just received a grant from the U.S. government to set up an office. Her purpose was to inform single senior citizens that we are the fastest growing segment of our population to contract venereal diseases.

Let me repeat that in case it didn't sink into your consciousness, because when I read it the first time I didn't comprehend the enormity of what I was reading either. Yes, it is true, single senior citizens are the fastest growing segment of our population to contract venereal diseases!

Stunned, I realized that since I'm over 55 and part of the single population of our country, she was writing to me. Even at my age I could be vulnerable to contract venereal disease if I was sexually active! Although I personally don't have to worry about that possibility, I fear for other Savvy Singles who are as innocent, or should I say ignorant, as I was before reading the article.

The woman's story was a very sad one. Her husband had decided to leave his wife of more than 35 years for a secretary at the company where he worked. He filed for divorce. The wife unwillingly joined the ranks as a single senior citizen.

Some time later the husband decided that being single and chasing the women at work was not all he thought it would be. He asked his ex-wife if he could come home and try to put their marriage together again. She finally agreed.

He stayed only a few months and left again. But, he was there long enough to give her the HIV virus and now she has AIDS. As she said in the article, sadly she won't have the joy of seeing her grandchildren grow up.

This is a tragic story. Besides wanting to personally go after the guy and kick him, my heart really goes out to her, even though I've never met this lady.

Yet, I imagine I might have done the same thing and let him come back home. Women naturally want to fix things. We are nurturing; we take in stray puppies and, sometimes, strayed humans.

This article in the *USA Today* newspaper is one of the reasons I decided to write this book. There are many issues, such as venereal disease, that people our age don't even consider as part of our world.

As the article mentioned, one of the reasons venereal disease is so rampant in our age group is that many people, like the lady in the paper, have been married since high school or college. They have only had one partner all these years and venereal disease is not even part of their thought process.

There is also a marked increase in divorces between the ages of 55-60, many instigated by women who have been unhappy for decades, their children are gone, and they decide there must be something better they can do with the rest of their lives. Suddenly, they're single and realize they don't have to worry about getting pregnant—it's party time! It doesn't occur to them that such promiscuous behavior puts them at high risk of contracting sexually-transmitted diseases and even HIV/AIDS to say nothing of how it violates God's boundaries that clearly reserve sexual relations for marriage.

One friend of mine, Ken, who was on the board of a company where I also served, talked to me after his wife of 46 years died. Ken told me that he had dated his wife in high school and even though they didn't marry until after college, she was the only girl he had ever made love to.

As we talked, Ken laughed and said that one of his married friends was envious because now it was Ken's time to go out and experiment, try out lots of girls. The callous sound of their discussion made me cringe. Obviously it was to just have sex for self-gratification, not because he cared about the woman.

As the conversation continued, I was disgusted with Ken's cavalier attitude as he repeated again that his friends said to go out and get any girl he could. Now, I am not so naïve to believe no one thinks like that. I am sure many singles do. But, finally, in exasperation I blurted out, "Well, you have stupid friends!"

He was in shock as I continued, "What your friends haven't figured out is that any woman who would have sex with you, just to have sex, will sleep with anybody!"

Now, he was getting a little mad. "Ken, I'm not putting you down, but what you don't realize is that you are very vulnerable to pick up any venereal disease from the last seven guys she has slept with."

Ken was still sputtering so I told him about the article I read in the newspaper. "If you don't believe me, just go online. You will find more about venereal disease on the Internet than you really want to know."

SAFE OR SORRY

For many of us senior singles, we have had the joy, the comfort and the security of making love with our spouse for years. When sex was a wonderful part of our marriage, we miss it along with the companionship.

One Christian man to whom I was talking said, "Well, it would be different if we hadn't been married. If it feels good and both people are consenting, what's the big deal?"

For many people, sexual abstinence is just a religious rule that makes no sense. But the "big deal" is like any of the other guidelines in the Bible that God warns us about, God's restrictions and direction about saving sex for marriage is not only for our physical protection but our emotional protection as well.

I'm not little old church lady with her hair in a bun or a prude, and I don't believe God wants you to sound or appear that way either. But to remain healthy, we must approach dating as Savvy Singles with self-control, lovingly and not lustfully, and in submission to God. He will honor us.

My unofficial survey found that while some senior men have sex for the enjoyment of sex, most senior women "make love" because of their need to feel loved, wanted, and beautiful—to feel connected.

When my husband died some years ago, I had to make a decision. How was I going to handle the dating dilemma? I came across a book called *Boundaries In Dating* by Drs. Cloud and Townsend that talked about setting boundaries for ones self in the dating process. To be Savvy Singles, we must establish boundaries for ourselves, that are biblically based and are established in terms of what is right and what is wrong—boundaries that make us feel comfortable and protected.

Whether it is one of the more than two dozen Sexually-Transmitted Diseases (STDs) or HIV/AIDS, unfortunately, the real facts about using condoms for protection from venereal disease, has been proven wrong—they do not provide the protection needed. They do help but are not foolproof. The only proven, foolproof protection against venereal disease is abstinence.

While I am aware abstinence is not a popular position, it is a life or death choice. We must individually make that choice for ourselves.

When I say that abstinence is the only foolproof method of protection, I can hear groans. After all, perhaps you've been enjoying sex for some time now as a single person, and you haven't contracted any venereal diseases. But if you have had unprotected sex, you are playing Russian roulette with your life. You could contact it at any time. Unprotected sex is not smart.

Some years ago, Mary Ann told me her story. No, she didn't get HIV, but she contracted a venereal disease. It seems that Jerry, whom she had been dating for almost a year, had also been dating (and having sex with) someone else during that same time.

Mary Ann said she still remembers the hurt and betrayal she felt when he told her. She and Jerry were sitting on her balcony, having a cup of tea before going to dinner.

"Have you been dating anyone else," Jerry said casually, "while we have been going out?"

"Of course not!" Mary Ann quickly answered in shock.

"Well," Jerry said, "I hate to have to tell you this, but I went out a couple of times with another woman. I contracted a venereal disease from her, and I may have given it to you." Jerry paused, "My doctor told me I had to tell you so you can be tested and treated before it gets worse, if you have it."

Mary Ann could not believe he could treat it so casually, as though he was apologizing that he may have given her a cold.

Mary Ann's story is a good example of what can happen when the wrong choices are made regarding sex outside of marriage. She was truly fortunate that the disease Jerry passed along to her was treatable and that Jerry was at least honest enough to tell her about it. It could have been much worse. Many times women don't exhibit symptoms and it may be a long time before they discover the damage that has been. You are the only one who can decide the dating boundaries with which you are comfortable and will keep you safe.

Josh McDowell, a Christian writer and speaker who targets the youth in America, was talking to a group of teenagers when he said something quite profound for anyone, even we Savvy Singles as we re-enter the dating scene.

"Remember," Josh said, "a relationship doesn't go backward, unless you end it. If you stay in a relationship, it will always go forward. For instance, when you first meet, you may shake the other person's hand. Maybe in succeeding dates you begin to hold hands. Then further on, perhaps you hug. But once you have hugged, you never go back to just shaking the other person's hand. So in relationships, it is up to each person to decide what boundaries he or she wants to live with at each stage of the relationship."

Unfortunately, many women as well as men don't set boundaries for themselves until they are in a crisis. But boundaries are not like a fire alarm box that you break open in the case of emergency. Boundaries that work to keep you healthy are set in place early on—before the crisis.

Perhaps you're thinking as you read this chapter, that you haven't kept the boundaries, as you know you should have. You've even thought, how could I do what I know is wrong when I really do love Jesus, my Lord?

Well, you're not alone. Yes, even Christians, slip and fall into sin of one kind or another. Sin is sin. Isn't that what Peter did too? I don't think anyone loved Jesus more than Peter. But not even Peter's love for Jesus kept him from denying he knew Jesus when the situation was desperate.

Like Peter we ask ourselves in anguish, I *do* love Jesus, how could I have done this? How could I have failed Him? Yet, even in our failure and devastation, Jesus holds out His hand of forgiveness to us, encouraging us on our journey to honesty and wholeness, as He did Peter.

Boundaries help us become persons of honesty and openness. How we treat others as well as how we allow others to treat us will develop out of the basis of our boundaries. Boundaries should be woven into the fabric of our lives and are not limited to the issue of sex.

Many of us have had very stressful, negative past experiences in various areas of our lives. Without thinking about it, it is easy to be negative and loose hope in our senior years. It is easy to slip into believing that because our past has been difficult, these later years will be the same.

Not true! As a Savvy Single, we have the opportunity to change our negative attitude and indeed turn our disappointing life into a life of hope and joy and passion. There are so many good books available to encourage us in all phases of our lives. I've heard people say, well, I can't afford to buy a lot of books—go to the library. Or, instead of buying a new blouse, buy a new book. Decide to invest in yourself and retrain your mind, your conversation, and eventually, your life.

At the back of this book, I have included a list of books I recommend you read. Although they aren't books written specifically for us as Savvy Singles, they contain useful information for our journey.

When we establish boundaries that are comfortable for us, we won't have to make a big issue about them. They will simply define who we are. Boundaries will have a positive effect in all aspects of our relationships: socially, emotionally, sexually, spiritually, and all areas of life. As we reach out to others with joy, honesty, and responsibility, they will respect our boundaries, finding in us a person they will want to take time to know.

POINTS TO PONDER

❖ You must consider and face uncomfortable issues as part of your world.

❖ Approach dating with self-control, lovingly and not lustfully, to honor God and yourself.

❖ Abstinence is a life or death choice.

❖ You must decide your dating boundaries.

❖ Set boundaries before a crisis—and stick to them.

❖ Boundaries help you become a person of honesty and openness.

❖ Boundaries should be woven into the fabric of your life.

❖ Boundaries define who we are.

Chapter 7

MONEY LAUNDERING & FINANCIAL SENSE

Laundry has never been much of a problem for me. I learned how to do it from my mom, down in the basement of our house in the Dakotas. Although we had a water heater, for some reason it wouldn't heat enough to do all the laundry. My mom had a little stove with a pipe going out the basement window where she would build a fire and heat the water for the washing machine.

One of the important things I learned from Mom was to look in the pockets of my dad and brother Bob's Levi jeans before they were washed. This was so we didn't accidentally wash something that shouldn't be washed, and with my brother you never knew what you might find in his pockets.

"Money laundering" is a term often used these days for a "front" business through which illegal money is "laundered" or made to seem legitimate. In the whispers of society, it seems that money laundering pervades many areas.

But my kind of money laundering didn't bring me financial gain. I think that was why I was so disgusted with myself the day I laundered my own money. For some unknown reason I'd stuffed a couple of hundred dollar bills into my jeans after I cashed a check at the bank. That's so unlike me to be so careless with money, but that's what happened.

Upon taking the jeans out of the washer, I noticed a lump in the pocket. Reaching in, I found the soggy mess of hundred dollar bills. Thankfully I was able to smooth them out while wet, iron them and then take them back to the bank for new bills.

Wouldn't it be great if our money problems could be solved so easily? It would indeed be a wonderful world if I didn't have to write this chapter about potential money problems. But in today's world of broken promises, it's important to have a clear understanding about financial matters before entering into a marriage, how they will be handled after the vows are spoken, and how assets will be protected in the event the marriage ends. With the climbing divorce rate near 50 percent, a Prenuptial Agreement is important to have, especially if it's not your first marriage and there are children involved.

I realize this isn't a popular subject in Christian circles. Even my own pastor expressed doubts about the need for such a legal document. He has been married to his precious wife for over 30 years. They married young and have built their family and assets together. In their generation and situation, such an agreement isn't needed. However, when I shared with him some examples of what's happening in today's culture with marriages that occur after the death of a spouse or divorce and the complicating risk factors involved, he saw it in a different light.

I'm sure we all agree with the wisdom of preparing a will to disperse assets after death. A Prenuptial Agreement simply does the same thing in the event of the death of a marriage, which unfortunately happens in Christian families at the same rate as unbelievers. A prenuptial agreement also provides a road map, as to how finances will be handled in the marriage.

Now the information in this chapter is in no way a treatise on "Prenups," nor will it take the place of having your own attorney draw one up for you. Instead, the purpose is to help us look at various pitfalls if an agreement is not written properly.

Living in the Palm Springs area of California as I do, with our many 50+ citizens, I've heard some sad tales of improperly written Prenuptial Agreements, or the lack thereof. As I travel around the country speaking at women's seminars, women like Sally share many of the pitfalls regarding such issues with me. Here is her story.

Sally's husband had been dead for some years when she met Harry through a friend in her bridge group. This is a different story from the movie "When Harry met Sally," but in the reality of today's culture it could very well be a sequel.

Harry was new in town, and he told Sally that his wife had died some years previous also. They immediately fell in love and had a whirlwind courtship. Harry said he had never met anyone like Sally and wanted to get married right away, as he said, "Before anyone else snatches you away."

Sally's husband had worked hard and with proper financial planning she had enough resources to take care of herself. In her discussions with Harry, he indicated that he had been very successful and had sufficient monies to take care of her. He said that she wouldn't need to use her own money once they were married.

Sally brought up the idea of having a Prenuptial Agreement, and Harry agreed, saying his children would be relieved to know they had one. He had his attorney draw one up for the two of them.

When Sally reviewed the Prenup, she saw that it protected Harry from her having any claims to any of his assets, but it didn't say anything about Sally's assets. That didn't bother her as she totally trusted Harry and believed his word was good.

When she showed it to a long-time businessman friend of hers, Glenn pointed out to Sally that there was no protection for her assets or method of payment for her if Harry ended the marriage. While that was true, Sally reasoned that she had her own money. Harry had verbally promised to pay for everything while they were married so she didn't have to worry. But as Glenn pointed out, even the promise to pay for her expenses and take care of her was not in the Prenup. She had no protection.

As I stood in the large auditorium looking at Sally's broken countenance, I really didn't want to hear the rest of her story.

"I can't believe I was so stupid," she continued tearfully, "I thought we really loved each other and would have a wonderful marriage."

At the urging of her friend, Sally did take the Agreement to her attorney. After reading it over, he asked to meet with the two of them. Harry was somewhat reluctant but finally agreed to go. When Sally's attorney explained that he was concerned for his client, Sally, and that there was no protection for her should the marriage not last, Harry asked, "Just what do you mean, exactly?"

"Well," the attorney explained, "while I see you have protected your assets from any claims, there needs to be some kind of protection for Sally's assets as well as some kind of payment for damages to Sally should the marriage not last more than, perhaps, a couple of years."

"I'll never pay anyone anything like that!" Harry exclaimed. Angrily shifting in his chair, he said, "If Sally can't trust me to take care of her, then we have no basis for a marriage. I, sir, am a man of my word!"

Looking at Sally's stricken face, her attorney said he would like to speak to Sally privately. When they were alone, he told Sally she should not sign the Prenup until it was properly revised.

"I really appreciate your concern," Sally replied, "but Harry really is an honorable man and I'm sure I can trust him."

"I know you believe Harry, but I've seen this happen too many times," her attorney said, looking at her with concerned eyes, "you really do need some kind of protection. If he won't provide for it in the Prenup, then maybe he isn't the kind of man you think he is."

But, as Sally recounted, she had not taken into consideration his grown family who were all involved in the family business. Whether it was out of misplaced loyalty to their mother or simple greed, they didn't want their father to marry anyone, no matter who it was.

"After only three months of pressure," Sally was crying by now, "Harry caved in to their demands and ended the marriage. I couldn't believe he would do this. He said he was very happy in our marriage, but couldn't be responsible for his family being destroyed, whatever that meant."

When he ended the marriage, he said he didn't feel obligated to reimburse Sally for any expenses. After all, it wasn't like she had any house payments during that time. Sally owned her home outright and that was where they were living after they married.

"But," Sally continued, "I think the worst part of it all was that he treated me like someone he could just dismiss out of his life, on a whim, because his family wanted him to. I was so embarrassed in front of my friends."

As I sensed Sally's broken spirit, I wished I could just wrap her up in my arms and tell her it was OK, but it wasn't. She not only had to live with the embarrassment of a divorce, but the cost of the divorce substantially impacted her savings as well.

I wish I could say her situation was unique, but it's not. This kind of story is repeated in a variety of forms all across our nation. Unfortunately, it's usually women who get the short end of the deal. Men are more accustomed to working with contracts and used to protecting themselves in business as well as protecting their assets. Most women are too trusting, especially when they are in love.

DOLLARS AND SENSE

I remember one businessman friend telling me, just before I entered into a business agreement, "Samantha, make sure the contract has a provision for ending the agreement in case your business relationship doesn't work out, for any reason. You'll probably never have to use it, but when you haven't clearly spelled out how to end the business relationship, if you need to get out, then you'll have a mess."

Thankfully, I followed his advice as that business relationship didn't work out. Yet, because of the prior provisions in the contract, we were able to sever our business relationship and still remain friends.

I think that's good wisdom for a Prenuptial Agreement as well. Hopefully, you'll never have to use the provisions, but if you do, they are there.

What are some of the obvious pitfalls Sally could have avoided? First of all, when both her friend and her attorney pointed out that she was not protected, she should have heeded their advice. There is wisdom in a multitude of counselors. If her fiancé was not willing to put in writing what he had promised to her, what was it worth? Nothing. Sally learned the hard way something businessmen understand is true—if it's not in writing, it means nothing. Insisting that everything be spelled out is not lack of trust but rather an intelligent decision to protect both people.

Another caution sign should have been when he became so upset that he would be required to put in writing that he would pay damages to Sally if the marriage didn't work out. It should have shown her the truly stingy spirit of this man she thought she knew so well.

Money is always a difficult subject in a marriage. Money is widely considered one of the top reasons for divorce, and it isn't just the lack of it. Many times it's disagreement about how and by whom the finances are being handled in the marriage. If finances can't comfortably be talked about *before* marriage, it isn't going to get any better later.

"Remember, when you're dating, this is as good as it's going to get," my Pastor, Fred, said in a sermon on marriage. "Each of you will be wanting to please the other, be more charming and fun than you will after the reality of marriage settles in. So ask yourself, is this relationship enough, as it is? It isn't going to get any better."

Depending on the financial stability of each person, there are a variety of ways people today are working out their finances pertaining to marriage. If both people come into the marriage with assets, one prevalent solution is for each to pay into a joint account a percentage of their living expenses based on their individual assets. For instance, if one person has four times as much as the other, that person would put in 75 percent of the money needed for their living expenses and the other person would put in 25 percent.

The benefit to this plan is that they are not mingling funds, which most financial advisors are adamant about. In today's world of finances and tax laws, this is an important consideration. You need to talk to your CPA and your attorney. They will be aware of the laws applicable in the state in which you live.

I have known couples who, because the man had a much larger estate than the prospective wife, decided that he would indeed pay for all of the living expenses. If this is what the couple chooses, then it needs to be stated in the Prenuptial Agreement.

Another couple I know agreed that the man would pay for all of the living expenses except her clothes and her telephone. So, as you can see, there are as many solutions to handling money issues, as there are people. No one way will work for everyone. As long as there is clear, mutual agreement, put it in writing so there is no misunderstanding.

It's also important to know how state laws may impact your finances when you marry. Tom and Julia lived in a state with community property laws. Both had been divorced and both were successful freelance business professionals. Although Julia had been living separately from her husband for several years, her divorce was finalized in January 2001. Tom and Julia were married in September of 2001.

In the spring of 2002, Tom and Julia began preparing their 2001 income tax returns. Tom had lived in another state until recently and just assumed they could file their taxes separately since this was their first year of marriage. It would be simpler to keep their business assets separated that first year since they were only married for less than four months out of the twelve.

However, after talking with their CPA, Tom and Julia were in for a big surprise due to community property laws in the state in which they were married and were residing. Since Julia was still legally married in January 2001 to her first husband, who was a very wealthy businessman, the 2001 assets of her first husband had to be calculated into Julia's taxable income.

Also, in this state it wasn't possible for Tom to file his return totally independent of Julia's since they were married in 2001. By the time the taxable income of Julia, her first husband, and Tom were pooled together; their tax rate was in the highest bracket possible. Tom was horrified. Had they been aware of how the state laws would impact their assets, Tom and Julia would have waited and married in 2002.

I can't stress enough how important it is to talk about finances before marriage. Savvy Singles need to know how each person views spending and investing. If one is a spendthrift and the other is a penny pincher, trouble looms in the wings. If one is a very conservative investor and the other goes after the high-risk portfolios, a balance must be reached regarding investment strategies.

Singles who have had independence in handling their own finances must be willing to adapt to a spouse's views and habits. If discussions about money always end up in an argument or if no resolutions are made, take it as a danger signal.

How do you feel when you go out to dinner? Are you comfortable with the types of places you go and the amount of money spent? Go shopping together often and observe how decisions are made about purchases. Are your lifestyles compatible with regard to spending? If you don't like the way your prospective spouse handles money, don't remain silent. It won't get better after marriage.

Here are some issues that should be considered and included in a Prenuptial Agreement per the advice of legal counsel for both parties:

1. A statement of who will contribute what to the family expenses, or what percentage of the individual incomes.

2. If the two parties are from different states, be sure that the requirements of each state are fulfilled and that the differences are clearly understood. Be sure to look at the tax consequences.

3. An agreement on the means of supporting any children or a spouse of a former marriage or other dependent relatives.

4. Prepare tax and financial statements for clear disclosure of properties and assets prior to marriage.

5. An agreement of how premarital property, owned singly or jointly, will be divided if there is a divorce.

6. An agreement of what happens to any property or assets acquired jointly during the marriage.

7. Define what happens to a business partnership between a husband and wife if the marriage is dissolved.

8. A statement indicating whether the wife intends to use her new married name.

9. Instructions on how the agreement can be terminated or altered or if there is an ending date to the binding of the agreement.

These are just a few recommendations. Please consult your attorney for more detailed legal advice.

To summarize: Savvy Singles face financial issues up front and with honesty. Savvy Singles ask the right questions and analyze the answers, not with emotions, but rather by applying good financial sense. Savvy Singles avoid money laundering and take the proper action to protect assets. How savvy are you with regard to your finances and relationships? Take heart, we're all learning and growing one day at a time.

POINTS TO PONDER

❖ Have a clear understanding about financial matters *before* entering into a marriage.

❖ A Prenuptial Agreement protects both people.

❖ There is wisdom in a multitude of counselors.

❖ Money is one of the top reasons for divorce.

❖ Talk about finances before marriage—it won't get any easier later.

❖ Know how state laws may impact your finances when you marry.

❖ Savvy Singles need to know how each person views spending and investing.

❖ Arguing about money signals future disaster.

Chapter 8

BUILD A LIVING NETWORK

Sue Ann Wilding is not her real name, but it will do for this story. When she was young, she was a part-time actress in Hollywood. Today, she is an alcoholic who doesn't admit it. Sue Ann keeps her hair, make-up, and clothes quite carefully; and with her biting humor and loud laugh, she is always noticed in a crowd. Because of her erratic behavior as well as caustic tongue, she has chased away most of her acquaintances and now lives as a lonely old drunk. She would be shocked to know we all thought that about her.

In recent years, Sue Ann has often times called me to take her to the bank or to pick her up from the hospital emergency room. Since I frequently travel out of the area, most of the time Sue Ann calls a mutual friend, Elaine, to help her.

One day she called Elaine and sounded very disoriented, not even knowing where she lived, obviously in need of help. Elaine convinced Sue Ann to call 911. She did, but was released from the hospital after a few of hours. Apparently they get a lot of poor souls in that condition and there is only so much they can do. So she left the hospital and that was the last we heard of her for a week.

Sue Ann had not returned home but her car, however, was parked at her home. We filed a missing person's report but the police didn't seem concerned. They had a file on her three inches thick from all the times when she had called them while hallucinating that someone was trying to break into her home or rape her. Of course, when they arrived, they found no indication anything was wrong, except that she was drunk.

Our problem was that we didn't have a name or phone number of her brother in the Los Angeles area or of her stepson in Paris. We didn't know a relative to call or have any way to make sure she was OK.

As I mentioned in an earlier chapter, people today don't have the built-in support system they did during biblical times or even years ago when people lived in smaller communities. Three and four generations don't live in the same house or compound or even the same community as they used to do. As Savvy Singles, whether we live in a city or in the Sun-Belt, often we have no one who daily checks on us except maybe for our friends.

While Sue Ann's situation may seem an extreme example, albeit true, about why we need to build a network, it is none-the-less important. I'm not talking about the kind of network you build in business when you collect business cards, and now e-mails, so you can contact people on your way to success. No, this is a simple, day-to-day Living Network.

Living in a retirement area as I do, we become aware of the multiplied thousands of people who live somewhere other than where they grew up. And their families often live hundreds if not thousands of miles away.

As we get older, our area of influence diminishes, due simply to aging and the nomadic tendencies of Americans. Thus, a Living Network becomes all the more important, especially for Savvy Singles who live alone without a family support system nearby.

Whether the problem is an illness, accident, earthquake, hurricane, flood or tornado; disasters, large and small, do happen. With some simple preparation, at least we will have the help we need and our loved ones will be notified.

CREATE A NETWORK

If you have e-mail access, you can set up your network in a matter of minutes, though you do need to be careful about what information you send in addition to contact names and phone numbers. While you can set up your network by phone, it is much more accurate if you write the information and either send it by e-mail or by snail-mail.

Here is how to set up your Living Network:

1. Make certain you have a card in your wallet or purse that clearly states who to call in case of an emergency. For example: In Emergency Call: Jane

Doe at 555-234-5678. You should have two names on the card, in the event one is not at home.

2. Tell the people listed on the emergency card that you have listed them as your point of contact. Make sure these emergency contact people and some of your other local friends have names and phone numbers of your close friends and family members living in other areas, as well as your doctor's phone number.

3. Make sure your distant family and attorney (if applicable) have the names and phone numbers of your support system of friends where you live. Remember to include your local doctors, attorney, and perhaps your pastor.

I can imagine you are thinking, but I'm not a drunk and I certainly don't hallucinate. That may be true, but you might fall down or have a car accident or have some other need. The more informed your support system—Living Network—the safer you will be.

We also need to encourage our younger, working families who live away from childhood homes, to set up the same Living Network with distant family.

Just as I was working on this chapter, I received a call from my sister, Ruth. It seems that her younger son, Rich, was driving on a loose gravel road in the Dakotas and he overturned his truck. Someone found him, and he was taken to the hospital with a broken back. It was two days before he could talk and tell them to call her. He didn't have any emergency phone numbers in his wallet, so the hospital didn't know whom to call. So much could have happened in those two days by himself, not able to talk.

In addition to putting an emergency contact card in your purse or wallet, it would be wise to put one in the glove compartment of your vehicle too.

People who have life-threatening illnesses such as diabetes should especially have that type of information available for others to find. They may pass out and the authorities may think they have been drinking alcohol and not seek the medical attention that is needed. All Savvy Singles should understand the importance of immediate information in times of emergency. If you have a life-threatening illness be sure to wear an identification bracelet and put this information on the emergency contact card in your wallet.

Some emergency services have a standard recommended procedure for where people should place critical medical or contact information in their homes. In case ambulance, police, or fire personnel are called to the residence, they know exactly where to find the information. For example, some use a special vial that is placed in the refrigerator listing the doctor's name, life-threatening medical conditions, such as diabetes, a list of prescriptions being taken, name and phone number of next of kin, etc. Call your local emergency agency and ask if they have such a procedure and then follow their instructions.

The next section of this chapter is a separate action but part of your Living Network— helping your loved ones function more easily in times of emergency.

FAMILY FRIENDLY

In light of new laws that have been passed regarding privacy of medical information, such as the HIPPA legislation, it is more important than ever that Savvy Singles have a durable power of attorney for medical and financial affairs in the event you are incapacitated. The new laws make it almost impossible for family members to find out what is taking place if you are in an accident or become suddenly ill. Many people don't realize that a general power of attorney for handling financial affairs becomes null and void if the person becomes incapacitated.

Mary shared with me what happened when her mother, who lived in a distant state, suffered a stroke. A caregiver who came in each day found Mary's mother, Helen, on the floor and called 911. The ambulance came and transported Helen, who was conscious and talking but with some mild impairment, to the hospital. The caregiver called Mary to let her know what had occurred but at that point didn't know the extent from a medical perspective.

Mary called the hospital and was unable to get any information about her mother. When Mary informed the nurse that she did have a signed durable power of attorney and was the designated person in the document to act in her mother's behalf, she was told to fax the document to the hospital. Even then she had great difficulty getting information from the nurses on the critical care unit throughout the night until she could make flight arrangements to be at her mother's side. Upon speaking with the doctors at the hospital after her arrival, Mary was told that her mother had suffered a major stroke and was paralyzed on her left side.

Without that signed power of attorney document, the situation would have been impossible for the family. Even with the document in hand, Mary still battled with the hospital staff the entire time she was at the hospital with her mother trying to get information and see that the proper care was rendered.

Since Helen was a widow of only two months, Mary had to handle all of the affairs of her father's estate and pay her mother's bills, etc. It had taken several years to convince her mother to have a durable power of attorney prepared and signed. Even then, because of her determined independent spirit, Helen refused to give Mary a copy of the document until just few months before her stroke. We have to realize how difficult we make it for our loved ones if we don't prepare for emergencies and face the realities of what can happen.

Another matter we Savvy Singles often don't want to talk about is a Living Will or what should be done in the event of a terminal illness regarding "Do Not Resuscitate" orders. This is a very personal matter but it is important to discuss this with your family members, especially whomever you designate as your representative in the durable power of attorney document.

LOCATION, LOCATION, LOCATION

Where you keep your important documents and records is another issue we Savvy Singles must address in the event of emergencies. Even in our age of computers, there is merit in keeping old-fashioned paper records of the important information of our lives. I must admit, even though I am quite an organized person, until I started research on keeping systematic records all in one place, I never thought of its crucial importance.

Professional organizers encourage their clients to keep a paper trail. Not only do we need this information all in one place, but if we have aging parents, we need it for them too. Yes, many Savvy Singles have parents in their 80s and 90s who may need help setting up a Living Network.

To keep a Network Notebook, buy a three-ring notebook with alphabetical dividers. Then you can list important information alphabetically; enabling your loved ones to easily find the information they need. There are also three-ring pocket inserts that can be added behind the dividers that will hold copies of any important documents. Additional pages can be added to sections as needed. If you would like to see the one I use, visit my Website at www.samanthalandy.com.

You will want to include the following contacts and information, customizing it for your needs. Include the names, phone numbers, e-mail and home/business addresses for the following:

1. Accountant(s).

2. Attorney(s).

3. Doctor(s).

4. Family members (these should probably be in a separate section).

5. Friends (these should probably be in separate section too).

6. Neighbors.

7. Pastor(s).

8. A list of all medical conditions known and current medications being taken along with the name and phone number of the pharmacy.

9. Car insurance policy numbers as well as agent contact information.

10. Health insurance policy numbers and phone numbers.

11. Homeowner's or renter's insurance policy numbers and phone numbers.

12. Investment banker's name(s), addresses, and phone numbers.

13. Hair salon or barber shop information.

14. Birthdays listed by month (if many grandchildren and friends, you may want this in a separate section of your directory).

15. Home repair contacts and phone numbers.

16. Poison control phone number.

17. Police non-emergency phone number.

18. School (if applicable) names and phone numbers.

19. Work (if applicable) names and phone numbers.

This is far from being a complete list, but it gives you an idea of what your Network Notebook should contain. When you have your notebook complete, or are working on it, be certain to inform family members, near and far, who need to know about it, where it is located. Ideally, it should be kept in a drawer near a phone for quick use in emergencies.

"CAN YOU HEAR ME NOW?"

Maybe the following is one of the most important parts of this chapter. I hope everyone will heed the advice. *Every senior adult who is single needs to have a cell phone.*

While I find it most helpful to be able to call and tell my friends I will be ten minutes late for our luncheon appointment, you may not see the necessity for that. But don't do what Marian, an older friend of mine, does. She keeps her phone with her but says she only uses it for emergencies, so it is never turned on nor do any of us have her number. What she doesn't realize is that her family, living in other states might want to reach her in a hurry for an emergency, and her phone is not on. What she also doesn't realize is that in an emergency, time is critical. It takes time to boot up a cell phone. Therefore, it's better to leave it on, so it is ready when needed.

Even if we choose not to give out our number to people, it's important to give it to family members and one or two close local friends. Also, be sure to have important numbers programmed into your cell phone so you can make calls quickly. If you can't figure out how to program the phone numbers, find someone who is more technically savvy to do it for you. This is part of the Living Network we need to keep us safe.

The other thing that I believe every single adult needs is to have a travel assistance membership, such as AAA roadside service. Even if you have your vehicle insurance with another company, you can still be buy AAA roadside service for a minimal cost. AAA doesn't pay me anything to recommend them, but with all the traveling we all do, AAA seems to be the best and most available across the country. If you have a flat tire or other roadside emergency, it's not prudent to wait for some traveler to help us.

If you have a cell phone, you can dial the number on the back of your card and get help immediately. (The number can also be programmed into the cell phone directory along with other important numbers.) In today's world we just can't trust strangers to be good and kind and not take advantage of us.

MUM'S THE WORD

This section is very important for Savvy Singles who have people in and out of their home, such as cleaning people, healthcare people, repair people, and others. These people should *not* have access to the numbers and information listed below.

You may want to designate an adult child to have this information, or a trusted friend of many years or perhaps your attorney, if you've known them for a long time. Choose very carefully; but someone you trust does need to have it in case you are unable to take care of things yourself. Keep your own copy in a secure place.

1. Alarm system information.
2. Banking information (list accounts, account numbers and location).
3. Computer passwords.
4. Credit card account numbers.
5. In-house safe keys or combinations.

6. Safety deposit information.

7. Location of durable power of attorney documents with the name of the person designated and phone number.

8. Location of Last Will & Testament (name of attorney and where document is stored).

9. Documents or information regarding prepaid funeral and burial arrangements.

10. Life insurance policy.

Rather than have too many people with access to such personal information, you may want to give instruction as to who has the information. For instance, next to the Safety Deposit Box, you might indicate—Contact Jim XXX, my son, Phone #_____. Then make sure that you've given that person the information.

Emergencies can happen to any one of us at any time. Build your Living Network and Network Notebook and get a cell phone now! Stop reading, build your network and then come back to this book. We'll both feel better.

POINTS TO PONDER

❖ A Living Network provides relief for you and your loved ones.

❖ A Living Network makes you feel safer.

❖ Keep emergency phone numbers in your purse, wallet, and your vehicle.

❖ Check with your community EMS for standard recommended procedures.

❖ Preparation now means less stress and heartache for family and friends.

❖ Tell those who need to know where you Network Notebook is located.

❖ Every Savvy Single needs a cell phone.

❖ Every Savvy Single needs a good roadside emergency service.

Chapter 9

I BOUGHT A CONDO, WHERE?

"You can't imagine, Samantha, how devastating this past year has been," Jennifer almost whispered. Standing in line at the Post Office, I couldn't believe how much she had aged since I had seen her about a year ago. Whatever it was, it must have been truly devastating.

"I'm sorry, I don't know what's been happening," I anxiously replied.

"How it happened, I have no idea, but someone stole my identity. I didn't find out about it for almost six months, and when I did, it was almost a fluke."

"How could this happen?"

"Well, somehow they got a credit card number and ended up getting my Social Security number. Then they applied for new credit cards and put new addresses on the cards so everything went to their Florida address."

Jennifer's voice had elevated to a higher pitch by this time from all the stress. When I met her that day at the Post Office, she had been working on straightening out the mess for over four months. She had spent considerable money on attorney's fees and invested countless hours of her own time with all kinds of agencies, trying to get her good credit back. The people who had stolen her identity had purchased a condo in Florida using her credit as well as charged untold items on various cards. It was a mess. No wonder she had aged.

I wish I could say this was a rarity and almost never happens but it happens much more than we imagine. It also happens to a higher percentage of people over 55 than any other age group. Identity theft criminals know that we often have a higher disposable income than younger working people—or is it because we are not as savvy about protecting our records?

After hearing Jennifer's story, I casually made an inquiry of many of my single friends, and I was appalled to find out that I was almost the only one who had a paper shredder and used it. Whether we're single or not, we should all use a paper shredder to protect our identity. They are now so reasonably priced, compared to the cost of trying to undo an identity theft mess, they are in fact, very cheap.

As I was preparing to write this chapter, I was on my way to Seattle and flipping through the Alaska airlines in-flight magazine. Suddenly staring me in the face were these shocking statistics:

FACT - In 2002, nearly 10 million people were victims of identity theft.

FACT - On average, identity theft victims spend 175 hours of their personal time and over $800 to clear their names.

FACT - The FTC estimates it takes victims 14-to-16 months to clear their names.

Now, granted this was an advertisement for Fellowes™ Shredders, but the facts are still the facts. We need to protect ourselves from unscrupulous people.

It's important to shred those pre-approved low-rate credit card offers. Think how easy it is for someone to use those forms. Your credit has already been established, all they have to do is apply, change the address and viola! They have a new card, on your credit. If you don't shred them, there is a new breed of criminals out there called, "Dumpster Divers" who will retrieve them from your trash.

If you are buying a new shredder, the very best kind is called a cross-cut or confetti shredder. An identity thief can put the documents from a typical ribbon shredder back together with a little work. While the confetti shredder is a little more expensive, it's worth it as it makes your documents impossible to read.

Another important step is to cancel all of your unused credit card accounts. Not only does too many credit cards, even if unused, lower your credit rating, but the account numbers are often listed in your credit report and can be obtained by identity thieves.

I recently received an e-mail concerning identity theft written by an attorney who suggested we pass it along to our friends. It had some very practical advice, some of which I am including in this chapter.

Here are some ways to protect against identity theft:

- ❖ The next time you order checks have only your initials (instead of first name) and last name put on them. If someone steals your checkbook, they won't know if you sign your checks with just your initials or your first name, but your bank will know.

- ❖ Put your work phone number on your checks instead of your home phone or better yet, no phone number! Use a PO Box instead of your home address if possible.

- ❖ *Never* put your Social Security number on your checks, you can write it on if necessary. Your Social Security number should be guarded carefully. Don't give it out unless absolutely necessary.

The attorney who wrote the Internet article explained that his wallet had been stolen and within the week the thieves ordered an expensive monthly cell phone package, applied for a new Visa credit card, had a credit line approved to buy a Gateway computer, purchased thousands of dollars of clothes, received a new PIN number from the Department of Motor Vehicles to change his driving record information, and much more.

Interestingly, only months after I received this e-mail, I had my wallet stolen. So I retrieved the e-mail and followed directions. In addition to canceling my credit cards that very night, the e-mail recommended I file a police report. Since I only had a small amount of money in the wallet at the time, the police said it was still good to file the report because if they find the cards on someone they arrest for another reason, then there is a police record and they would also be charged with stealing my wallet.

But what is perhaps most important (I would never think to do this) call the three national credit-reporting organizations immediately to place a fraud alert on your name and Social Security number.

The attorney said he had never thought to do this until his bank called to tell him an application for credit was made on the Internet in his name. Filing this alert means that any company that checks your credit knows your information was stolen, and they have to contact you by phone to authorize new credit.

Here are the important numbers to call:

- ❖ Equifax: 1-800-525-6285
- ❖ Experian (formerly TRW): 1-888-397-3742
- ❖ Trans Union: 1-800-680-7289
- ❖ Social Security Administration Fraud Line: 1-800-269-0271

Another good resource to keep handy is The Identity Resource Center, a nonprofit organization established to help victims of identity theft and other scams. The Website is www.idtheftcenter.org.

ON-LINE SAVVY

Now, as if that's not enough to be concerned about, we also have to be alert to on-line scams that are very clever.

Another new type of criminal we need to watch out for is a "Phisher." The scam works like this: you get an innocent looking e-mail that appears to be from your Internet provider asking you to update your credit card information. So you fill out the form with your information. *Don't do it!* Call your Internet provider and, only if necessary, update your information verbally.

This scam happened to Patty and with a single "Enter" click she had unwittingly sent a 17-year-old computer whiz full access to her Visa account, which had a $25,000 spending limit. The boy had created a Web page identical to the Internet service provider's billing center page, produced bogus e-mails and gone phishing, as the new scam is known in on-line circles. The Phishing e-mails will say that you need to update or verify your account information. Be aware that your bank and on-line companies will never ask for this information in this way.

In 2003 and 2004, such phishing e-mails have reached the in-boxes of as many as 5 million on-line users. This has become such a huge problem that there is now a group established to combat it called the Anti-Phishing Working Group headed by David Jevans. According to Jevans, it seems there is a 52 percent increase in attacks each month.

Depending on what phishers do with your information, they can derail your financial life for years. Phishing and other forms of identity theft hit 10 million people in 2002 alone, costing them over $5 billion.

Here is a list of some possible scams to avoid.

I Bought a Condo, Where?

1. Never click on a link in an e-mail that requests financial or personal information. Telephone the company.

2. Bear in mind that businesses rarely need updates. If you gave information to a company once, it has it.

3. Don't respond to e-mail offers of merchandise at too-good-to-be-true prices or for free if you agree to a trial demonstration. These are favorite hooks for phishers. Offers are being posted on the Internet for items such as 42" flat-screen TVs and laptop computers. If you are willing to participate in a short-term marketing demo period, you get to keep the item for free. *Not!* The first thing that pops up on the screen is a form asking for your personal data.

4. If in doubt about an e-mail's authenticity, don't open it or call the company.

5. Trust me, you have *not* won a lottery in the Netherlands, or Canada or anywhere else if you didn't first buy a ticket for it here in the U.S.A. If you did, you don't need to give them money in order for them to process your winnings.

6. Beware of any company that offers you a prize but asks for a "shipping fee" or your Social Security number or a bank account number. They probably will never send your prize but they may steal your identity.

7. A stranger did not die and leave you money. They simply want information from you to string you along until you give them enough information to steal your identity or money from your bank accounts.

8. The "Nigerian Scam" has now morphed into all kinds of people writing and needing your help to transfer money from one foreign account to another. No matter how sincere they sound, this is money laundering and it is illegal. Recently, an e-mail has circulated from a "Christian" widow who is childless and dying of cancer. She wants to give her large estate to another "Christian." Don't even go there.

LISTEN FOR THAT STILL SMALL VOICE

While traveling with a girl friend in England, we almost got hooked into an illegal laundering scheme. We were in London in our hotel lobby when a very tall, nice looking man in jeans and cowboy boots asked if he could join us for tea. He said his name was Stuart and he was from Ireland.

It was fun talking to him about places to which we had all traveled and he invited us to join him for dinner at a nearby restaurant. He said he was leaving the next morning but would be back in London in a couple of days and again invited us to join him for dinner, as he hated to eat alone.

At the appointed time, we met Stuart at Trader Vic's Restaurant, one of my favorite places. During dinner he said he remembered that I mentioned my son had a jewelry business. Stuart explained that he had some old diamonds that had been in his family for many years. He needed them evaluated, but he just didn't know anyone in Ireland he could trust to grade them honestly for him. Since we looked like nice, honest people, he asked if I could take the diamonds back to the U.S. to have my son grade the stones and then mail them back to him.

Stuart gave me his business card that said he was an investment broker in Dublin. As the evening wore on that "still, small voice" in my spirit was not so small any more. There were just too many unanswered questions such as why a successful businessman did not have long-time friends he could trust. Finally I said, "You know, Stuart, I have a better idea about these diamonds. I will call my son and explain what you need. I know he will give me the name and phone number of the people he buys diamonds from in Belgium. He goes there a couple of times a year and knows they are very trustworthy. Then you can just fly over to Belgium yourself and get the stones evaluated. That would be the safest way to go."

Strangely, Stuart wasn't too excited about that idea. After again trying to get me to take the diamonds with me, he realized I wasn't going to do it and gave up. He didn't even stay for coffee saying he had another meeting. At least he paid for the dinner!

In thinking about that episode, I could see all kinds of ramifications such as the diamonds being stolen, to being arrested, on and on. Even though it was before 9-11 when there was less security, I didn't want to be caught smuggling diamonds.

Stuart thought we looked like two naïve women he could trick into helping him with a scheme. What he wasn't counting on was the "still, small voice of the Lord" that will talk to us and keep us out of danger if we listen.

SINGIN' THE BLUES

Another way to avoid scam artists is to buy a $2 blue gel pen. Over 20 years ago, my attorney told me I should never sign important documents with anything other than a blue gel pen. I have long forgotten all the reasons why, except for one. He told me that if there were ever a question about whether my signature was an original, if it was written with blue gel ink, it would be obvious. With the quality of copies today, it is impossible to tell whether a black ballpoint pen signature is an original or not.

Then, reading an article in a magazine, I found another reason we should always sign with a blue gel pen. All it takes to clean out your bank account is a signed check swiped from your outgoing mailbox. Here is how it's done.

The crook steals outgoing paid bills from your mailbox in front of your house. Then he places a piece of Scotch tape or other cellophane tape over the front and back of your signature on the check. Then he puts the check in a pan of nail polish remover for about 30 minutes. The nail polish remover removes anything that is not printer's ink, except for your tape-protected signature.

The company name you wrote the check to is gone. The amount written on the check is gone. They are left with a blank check and your tape-protected signature. The check is then blow-dried and flattened in a book. After that, the tape is carefully removed.

Guess what! They now have a blank check, signed by you.

In the true-story movie, "Catch Me If You Can," Leonardo DiCaprio gives a very explicit lesson on how to be a check forger and identity thief, including this process.

There is only one type of pen, a gel pen, that is counterfeit proof to acetone or any other chemical used in "check washing."

My favorite is the Uni-ball Gel Pen that is sold in office supply stores for about $2. It comes in rich blue ink, as well as other colors and in a couple of different point tips. The man played by DiCaprio in the movie, who now consults for law enforcement agencies about check theft, also recommends this particular pen.

So the next time you are writing out checks, get out your blue gel pen, knowing that when you're writing the name of the person or company you wish to have the check, as well as the amount, you are protecting yourself from check theft.

A $2 Uni-ball pen is a small investment for your protection; besides, they write very well. It's also my favorite pen for writing thank you notes (not done too much anymore, I admit) and sending them snail-mail.

A DIME A DOZEN

There are all kinds of other scams to watch for, such as additional fees tagged onto your on-line airline ticket or hotel reservation that pushes the total cost up. It is hard to discern this with so many additional security fees, fuel charges, etc. but if in doubt, ask.

Another widespread scam is car repairs—such as replacing oil filters, spark plugs, and other items for which you are charged but the services are not actually performed. Even a non-repair person like myself can easily check this. Simply put a felt-pen mark on an inconspicuous place on the item. If your marked item is still there and you were charged for the replacement, you've got a problem. A scam.

Another scam can occur regarding automobile manufacturer recalls. Joe recently shared that his SUV had a safety recall on the driver's seat. The recall had been issued several months before, but he hadn't taken time to take it to the dealership to have the replacement part installed. At a ballgame with some friends, one of the men reached up and used the back of the driver's seat to steady himself while getting out of the vehicle. The back of the driver's seat snapped completely off the base.

The next day Joe took the vehicle to the dealership along with the factory recall notice to have the faulty part replaced, which caused the back of the seat to separate from the base. The service manager informed Joe that according to the manufacturer's computer records this replacement part had already been installed at another dealership where Joe sometimes had service work done, and, therefore, he would have to be responsible for the seat repair.

Joe said that he had never taken the vehicle in to have this done nor had the dealership ever told him it had been done. The service manager had one of his crew check to see if the replacement had been installed, and the crewmember said he could find no evidence that the part had been replaced. The service manager recommended that Joe take the vehicle back to the dealership that had registered the replacement part and check out their claim.

Joe went to the service manager at the dealership that claimed to have replaced the part and told him quite emphatically that there was a problem. The service manager wouldn't admit that they had charged the factory for a part that was never installed, but he said he thought he could get the repair done under the "original" vehicle warranty.

The vehicle had 75,000 miles on it so it was unlikely the original warranty was valid. The repair didn't cost Joe any money, but it was obvious the dealership had scammed the factory and put in for a part that was never installed. It could have been a dangerous matter if that seat back had broken off and caused an accident.

Maybe one of the easiest places to get scammed is at the on-line auctions. My son Jim, who lives in Montana, loves eBay. His favorite deals are buying custom cowboy boots for a fraction of the retail cost. And yes there are great deals and great steals on the on-line auctions, including eBay.

But, anytime you get an offer from the seller that's outside the normal auction process, beware—it's a scam. Here are some additional on-line auction red flags you should avoid if you don't want to be scammed:

1. When the seller e-mails you and says you were not the winning bidder but they still have one more of that item to sell, and if you send a cashier's check, they'll send you the item. Usually, you never get the item, it was a scam and you bought it.

2. When the seller asks for payment through WesternUnion rather than Pay Pal.

3. When the seller won't accept such standard third-party payers like Pay Pal and instead asks you to use their own escrow company.

4. When the seller asks for your bank account numbers or Social Security numbers or information that is not required by Pay Pal. You should never give them out.

5. When the seller tells you they will ship items from an address or area other than the seller's address.

6. Maybe one of the easiest to spot, but unfortunately most successful scams, is when they ship from or are registered in, Andorra, a small country in the Pyrenees. It is well-known to be a home base for phony eBay vendors.

TEA FOR TWO

While I've never had the misfortune of identity theft, I have been involved in mistaken identity. It was quite fun and just so this chapter doesn't turn out to be a total "downer," I share my story of mistaken identity.

On one of my trips to London, England, I had the privilege of meeting with the Baroness Cox of Queensbury. She is the Deputy Speaker of the House of Lords and had been recommended as a possible speaker for the luncheon group I'm involved with in our desert area of California.

After numerous e-mails with her secretary, I was finally able to confirm an appointment while I was there. She said the Baroness could give me a half hour at 5:30 P.M. She invited me to tea at the House of Lords, England's governing body.

A navy suit and high heels was my choice of apparel, not wanting to look like a tourist in those august halls. I learned it is impossible to get into the House of Lords without a direct invitation from one of the Lords.

I arrived about 5:25 P.M., not wanting to keep the Baroness waiting. The guards at the door, who were all dressed in tuxedos, had me sit on a sofa near the entrance. At five minutes to six, I heard some commotion outside the entrance.

"If you're Samantha, come with me," the diminutive, striking dark-haired lady came running up to me saying, "I have to cast a vote on a bill. Can you run? We have to hurry!"

So here we were, running down the marble halls of the House of Parliament, me in my high heels, clicking along behind the Baroness. It was a long hall and people stopped to watch two crazy women running toward the chambers. Some of the guards in their tuxedos, just stood and watched, grinning. Apparently this wasn't the first time they had seen the Baroness running to vote. We made it just in time.

After she finished with her vote, we went in to the restaurant where they serve tea in the afternoon. We sat at a small table, overlooking the Thames River, watching the boat traffic drift by as we talked. The Baroness told me of some of her harrowing experiences traveling to third world countries setting up clinics and schools to help children.

"Oh, my goodness, I am late for my dinner appointment!" the Baroness said, two hours later as she suddenly looked at her watch. Once again, we hurriedly exited the restaurant. With a quick hug she was gone.

Since I wasn't in the hurry she was, I slowly walked down the long hall, looking at the magnificent statues, the gold carvings and at the stained glass windows high up in the ceiling.

"Excuse me, My Lady, I saw you with the Baroness. Are you new in the House of Lords? Is there anything I can do to help you, My Lady?" I turned and one of the "black tuxedos" stood before me, with his hands clasped behind his back, in a posture of respect.

Of course, when I giggled and spoke with my decided "Yankee" accent, he knew I definitely was not a member of the House of Lords. Nevertheless, we chatted for a few moments and he told me some of the history of various statues nearby.

Meeting my friends who were waiting in the car, I told them of my episode, and we all had a good laugh. Me in the House of Lords!

It started me thinking about the times I've been victimized by someone who looked good, conning me, making me think they were something they were not and cheated me out of money or used me in other ways such as opening up opportunities for them to meet certain people. Mistaken identity can be deliberate or a delightful episode such as the one I experienced in England.

Yes, clothes may make me look like a Baroness, but that's not all it takes to be a Baroness, that's for sure!

If you don't want someone buying a condo in Florida with your name and good credit, I hope you will apply what you have learned in this chapter. Unfortunately, there are many unscrupulous people who will take advantage of others, but the Lord told us in Matthew 10:16, *"Therefore be wise as serpents and harmless as doves."* We are to be wise in protecting ourselves from those who would try to steal from us and gentle in living our testimony of Christ-like love.

If you would like information about ordering a Savvy Singles Living Network Notebook to help you organize your important documents, look for my contact information at the back of the book. In the Living Network Notebook you will find pages with spaces for the same kind of list mentioned in the chapter. The notebook will help you gather the information you need for your family.

POINTS TO PONDER

- ❖ Use a paper shredder to protect your identity.

- ❖ Cancel all of your unused credit card accounts.

- ❖ Your Social Security Number should be guarded carefully.

- ❖ Call the three national credit-reporting agencies immediately if your wallet is stolen.

- ❖ Be alert to on-line scams that are very clever.

- ❖ Buy a $2 blue gel pen—or two.

SECTION THREE:

It's Back to Us

INTRODUCTION

If you have read this far in the book, congratulations! Do you realize that less than 10 percent of the people who buy a book actually complete it? With this statistic in mind, I can tell that you are serious about becoming a Savvy Single!

If there was any single chapter in the Bible that might be considered a roadmap for our lives as Savvy Singles, it could be Psalm 37. May I encourage you to read it often and make it part of your life? King David gives us good advice: *"Fret not yourselves because of evildoers," "Trust in the Lord," "Delight yourself in the Lord," "Commit your way to the Lord," "Rest in the Lord," "Cease from anger,"* on and on. (See Psalm 37:1,3,4,5,7,8.)

Then in verse 23, David assures us, *"The steps of a good man* [or woman] *are ordered of the Lord, and He delights in his way. Though he fall, he shall not be utterly cast down for the Lord upholds him with His hand."*

All through the Bible we see God enabling men and women to fulfill their destiny "in their old age." I think of Sarah, Abraham, Moses, Joshua, Dorcus, Paul, and John on the isle of Patmus. We have thousands of modern-day heroes like Grandma Moses who exhibited her first painting at age 80. Even President Reagan was considered an old man to hold the presidency, but he did a terrific job! Many scientists, with their wisdom and accumulated knowledge, have breakthroughs in their research in their latter years.

Thousands of people start whole new careers after they retire from their first career or from the military. Some become wonderful writers or painters or musicians, following dreams that may have been put on hold or put aside while raising a family or putting their children through college.

Consider the verse in Ephesians 5:15-16 (NASB), *"Therefore be careful how you walk, not as unwise men but as wise, Making the most of your time...."* And as it says in The Message Bible, *"So watch your step. Use your head. Make the most of every chance you get."* According to these Scriptures, age has nothing to do with who we are and what dreams we have. Based on these Scriptures, let us agree on this point, *"We gotta get our fire back!"*

Chapter 10

WE GOTTA GET
OUR FIRE BACK

In the book, *Alice In Wonderland*, Alice has a discussion with the Queen. "One can't believe in impossible things," said Alice.

"I daresay you haven't had much practice," said the Queen. "When I was your age, I always did it for half-an-hour a day. Why sometimes I've believed as many as six impossible things before breakfast."

That's whimsical, a fairy tale you say. But why is that? Why not believe in impossible dreams? They're only impossible if we never try.

Years ago I heard Oral Roberts say, "God will make the impossible, possible in an impossible hour." Of course, that wasn't just his idea; it came from the Bible. In three Scriptures

(Matthew 19:26, Mark 10:27 and Mark 14:36) Jesus said, *"With God **all** things are possible"* (my emphasis). It would seem, from my understanding of the English language, that "all things" also includes impossible things! In my life, and I imagine in yours, I have seen God do that—make the impossible happen.

"If our dreams can be accomplished without God's help, then our dreams are too small," I wrote in an article many years ago. I believe, in spite of our past history, in spite of what other people say, in spite of what we've experienced, God wants us to believe in big, impossible dreams. Such are His dreams for us. There have been so many times in my life that God has made the impossible, possible in an impossible hour. It's that unwavering trust in God to bring us through that sets up, in the spirit world, God's release of miracles in our lives.

"If we are obedient, God will move the farthest star or the smallest grain of sand to help us." This quote is from one of my favorite devotionals of Oswald Chambers. It brings me great comfort when I have a problem and can't see the way out. God will do whatever it takes to help me in my situation.

Maybe as a Savvy Single, your dreams were recently crushed or broken. Maybe your marriage didn't work out and now you're divorced, or maybe your spouse died and you still had plans and things you wanted to do together. Maybe your plans and dreams for your child's future didn't materialize like you thought they would. Whenever failed dreams and plans don't work out, the pain and devastation can linger for years.

If you are newly single or been at it awhile, maybe this is the time to take out your dusty old dreams that you had wrapped away so carefully in now-yellowed tissue paper in your mind. Maybe it's time to blow off the dust and evaluate what you want to do with your precious, laid aside or broken dreams.

The fact that you're reading this book makes me think you're ready to dream new dreams. Yes, it's time to begin again, whatever that means to you personally.

Viktor Frankl, author and Holocaust death camp survivor, wrote, "People do not lack strength; they lack will." Is that true for us? Because we are Savvy Singles, do we lack the will to dream again and take whatever steps are necessary to make our dreams come true? I hope not. Even the tiniest step toward a dream can be powerful.

This book is an example of choosing to dream again. I had wanted to write this book about dreaming and fulfilling our dreams as a single person, but I hadn't planned on making it a book for Savvy Senior Singles. However, as the years went by and I let other things get in the way of writing, suddenly I found myself categorized as a senior citizen.

Taking out my notes one day to begin writing, suddenly I realized I was writing it from a different perspective then when I had started collecting ideas and notes, years ago. I thought now that I am a Savvy Single, why not write it from this perspective. After all, we Savvy Singles need to fulfill our God-given dreams. Don't we? Maybe, just maybe, this is the perspective God wanted me to write from all along.

The same is true of your dreams and goals. Maybe the perspective you bring to your dream as a Savvy Single will have more meaning and impact with your increased wisdom and knowledge than it would have if you had accomplished your dream when you were in your twenties. Perhaps being sidetracked isn't so bad after all. You won't know unless you try.

IN THE BEGINNING WAS THE WORD

Let this be the day you write down a dream you would like to accomplish before a certain age. Set a goal. Then, map out step-by-step what events need to take place to begin the process toward accomplishing your dream.

There is great power in writing things down. The Bible bears witness to this truth as written in Habakkuk 2:2 NKJV:

"Write the vision and make it plain on tablets, That he may run who reads it."

The Lord was telling the prophet Habakkuk how important it was to write down the vision or dream so it wouldn't be forgotten over a period of time. God knew it would take a period of time before the prophecy would be fulfilled and He wanted the people to remember it clearly.

One day, I realized that verse applied to me too. If I write down my dreams and visions then I can run with them because they will be defined and I won't forget.

Motivational speakers like Zig Ziglar and others always say to write out our goals, plans, and dreams. Why? Because they have learned that the people who take the time to think about their dreams, visualize them, and write them down have a greater chance of actually doing them than those who just think about it. It also takes time for a goal or dream to be accomplished, and if it isn't written down, we won't remember what needs to be done to get there.

Take for instance this book. When I began collecting notes (some of which I never used) and writing down ideas, it gave my ideas substance. Then I came up with the working title, *Savvy Singles*. Even though I'm over 55, I'm not ready to be called a "senior," as I suspect many of you are not. But I liked the idea of being considered savvy and, of course, I'm single. So I put the title on my computer and made a notebook cover. That, too, gave my ideas power, it provided substance. So write your dreams down on paper or on your computer and keep them in a place you will look at them often.

Have you thought about writing your family history? I have met some remarkable seniors, and as I talk to them, I realize their grandchildren know little of the incredible successes they have had in life. They know little of their struggles and the lessons God has taught them. Even if you feel the publishing world wouldn't be interested in your book, your grandchildren and great-grandchildren would cherish this opportunity to know their grandparent and the life you have led. It would be a wonderful way to pass on your legacy of how God has brought you through to this point in your life.

There are numerous books available that will spur you on and give you a simple, easy-to-follow system. Does it seem overwhelming? Don't think of it as the daunting task of writing "the great American novel." Oh, me, oh my! But if you simply write one single page a day, at the end of the year, you'll have a 365-page book! Surely this is big enough to cover most people's life.

Yes, it's time to dream a new dream. I don't believe we were made to live an average, mediocre life. This doesn't mean we must be famous. Just a happy, successful human being, whatever that means to you.

We were made to soar; we were made to win. We can have the abundant life that Christ promised to us. Jesus didn't say the abundant life was only for a few select people. No, He offers it to each one of us. Jesus said in John 10:10, "...*I have come that they may have life, and that they may have it more abundantly.*" That's what Jesus offers to us, an abundant life, fulfilling our God-given dreams.

My mom, Anna, is an example of someone who fulfilled her dreams, maybe not in the way she planned, but she chose to fulfill them, accepting the limitations she had.

You see, her dream had been to be a schoolteacher. She came from a very large family, and there was no money for the girls in the family to get a college education. Now remember, this was in the Dakotas during the Depression and money was scarce. But she was determined. She found someone who was going to the town of Aberdeen, South Dakota, where the college was (200 miles away) and she asked if she could ride along. This person agreed. All she had was $10, two dresses, underwear, a coat, and one pair of shoes.

She found a job taking care of a professor's children and cleaning the house, which enabled her to go to school at night. She worked hard, maintained good grades, and was on her way to fulfilling her dream. Only one semester from her teaching degree, the professor and his family moved to another town. She couldn't find another job and had to return home without her teaching degree.

So, you ask, how could she fulfill her dream with no teaching degree? Well, my mom put her dream to use teaching Sunday school in the little church she attended. She was very busy with a large family of her own, but when she was close to her 40s, she agreed to teach Sunday school.

She loved teaching the preschool children and did so for 48 years! When she decided to step down, in her late 80s, it wasn't that she couldn't teach; her mind was very sharp up to the very end of her life.

"I just couldn't lift the little ones up to my lap when they needed a hug," she told me. "At their young age I couldn't explain to them so they would understand that I would like to lift them up but couldn't."

She ended up teaching two generations of children. Often when I went back to South Dakota and attended church with her, people would come up and talk to us, mentioning how much their child loved coming to her class. Many would say, "You know, I went to Anna's Sunday school class when I was a child as well. I remember how wonderful it was to be in her class so I'm not surprised my child loves it, too." What a heritage, what a wonderful example of fulfilling our dreams where we are in life.

Sometimes we can fulfill our dreams right now. Faith, my friend and hairdresser, is also fulfilling her dreams. She owns a very upscale, beautiful beauty salon. When she's working on a client, she doesn't take phone calls or talk to lots of other people—she gives each customer her full attention. She strives for excellence in every phase of her business. She has shared with me some of the many miracles God put in motion for her to have her salon and accomplish her dream.

Sometimes we get in a rut and settle for just OK, for average. Shake yourself out of your rut. Reach for your potential. Make plans to work better, be better next year. Good enough is not good enough for a child of the Most High God.

Randy, my younger son, was living a life of "good enough." He had been in the nuclear division of the Navy but hadn't used that knowledge after he was discharged. He worked at various jobs, including as a goldsmith in his brother's jewelry store, but I could tell he wasn't really excited about any of the jobs. I kept telling him he needed to find his own dream.

Finally, he decided to go to the university and get a Doctorate degree in pharmacy. Now over these last couple of years working as a pharmacist, he is living his dream. He is fulfilled, using the gifts and talents God has given him.

However, there may be times that no matter what we do, we encounter problems and setbacks, or what seems like a roadblock. No matter how hard we try, everything just disintegrates around us, and we are left with a pile of broken dreams or broken relationships.

But, as author Elizabeth Elliot says, "Every situation, if offered to God, can be our gateway to joy." We can offer to Him our pain, our disappointments, our disillusionment, our betrayals, our shame and our guilt; and He promises He will give us beauty for ashes.

Isaiah, when prophesying about the coming of the Messiah, said the Messiah would come,

> *"To console those who mourn in Zion, to give them beauty for ashes, the oil of joy for mourning, the garment of praise for the spirit of heaviness; that they may be called trees of righteousness, the planting of the Lord, that He may be glorified "*(Isa. 61:3).

Whether our pain and mourning is caused by broken dreams, divorce, or death of a spouse, Jesus the Messiah did not exclude those things. He simply read from the ancient prophet Isaiah the words of prophesy concerning Him, closed the book and said, *"Today this Scripture is fulfilled in your hearing"* (Luke 4:21).

Today, and every day for over 2,000 years, Jesus has been doing just that. He's been giving us beauty for our ashes, the oil of joy for our mourning if we but look to Him and trust in Him.

POLISHING OUR DREAMS

Just this morning, I was talking to my son, Jim, telling him of the tenacity it was taking to get this book written and edited and that I was giving up other things to accomplish my dream with this book.

Jim said, "Well, Mom, as the old ranchers around here often say, 'Get 'er done!'"

Jim knows about tenacity. He worked in a jewelry manufacturing company while in high school and then worked in jewelry stores during college. Now, he is living his dream of having his own jewelry store, which he opened a few years after college.

As I mentioned previously, he travels a couple times a year to Belgium to buy diamonds, and on one of his trips, I went with him. He asked me if I would like to see where they cut the really special diamonds. Of course I did.

He had to get clearance for me to get into the building. We went through all kinds of security doors with special codes and guards checking at each door. Finally we went up a rickety old elevator to the 6th floor. There were two more security doors. Then I had to leave my purse at the last door before I could go in.

Watching these men at their cutting tables, I was aware they were all quite old. By the time they work their way up to cutting the stones on the 6th floor, they have had lots of experience. It's here where the best gems are created.

The process of creating and cutting a diamond is quite incredible. It takes much skill and a sense of artistry for the gem cutter to be able to see the best cuts and facets for that particular stone. They have to know how to best show off the color and clarity of that gem.

Then, of course, there's the careful polishing that takes place. Obviously, you can't polish without friction, applied at just the right place and time. The final result is a beautiful gem, a sparkling diamond.

The whole process of choosing the stone, cutting, and polishing reminds me how it is in life. It's our problems and trials that God says He will use for our good. It's in the choices we make as we go through the issues of our life that brings out the beauty of our soul. Often we feel the broken dreams and pain of our past is a negative thing. But God truly can give us beauty for our ashes.

Some years ago I was teaching about Jesus giving us beauty for our ashes and encouraged the audience to take out their old dreams and work toward accomplishing them. Afterward a diminutive lady, Emily, came up to me.

"I think it is a lovely idea to work on fulfilling our dreams from the past," Emily said, "but you see, I always wanted to be a clown in the circus, and my parents wouldn't let me join the circus. Now here I am, a grandma, and I'm too old to be in the circus."

Looking in her tear-filled eyes, I could sense her sadness. To be reminded of her childhood dream but feel she could never do it was heartbreaking.

"What's the age limit to be a clown?" I asked, smiling.

"Well, I don't imagine there is any age limit to be a clown," Emily stared at me for a moment, "but I don't have a clue how to start."

By now I was really into this conversation, I wanted her to seriously think about the possibilities. "Well, you just go down to the costume store in your town, buy a big orange clown suit, put it on and stuff it with lots of tissue paper. Then get a pair of those big floppy shoes and a red nose. After that, you go down to the retirement home and tell jokes!"

By this time Emily's eyes were sparkling at the possibilities. "Maybe I will Samantha, maybe I will!" And she turned to go with new buoyancy in her step. Would she really try it out? I hoped so.

A few years later I was in her town again, speaking for another group. After the end of the session, I noticed a lady standing off to the side, waiting until all the other people were finished talking to me before she approached.

"Do you remember me, Samantha?"

Truthfully, I did not. It had been a few years since I had spoken in this town and hundreds probably thousands of people I had talked to in the interim years. I apologized saying I didn't recognize her.

"Well, I'm Emily, the Clown!" She nearly exploded with joy, "You said I should just be a clown even though I couldn't be in the circus."

Suddenly, I remembered the conversation, but this Emily had a zest and joy in her eyes that the other Emily didn't have. "So, tell me, what has happened."

"Well, it's so incredible." Emily laughed. "Since that time I have now become a Certified Clown and I have a regular time I go to the children's hospital and to the retirement homes. I'm even hired for children's parties! I'm having the time of my life! I'm so busy I have to turn jobs down!"

With that Emily hugged me saying, "Don't give up telling us it's never too late to fulfill our dreams, Samantha. I'm a certified example!" We laughed and hugged again with tears of joy.

And so I won't, I'll keep telling everyone it's never too late for your dreams. Get your fire back—be enthusiastic. A warm welcoming smile will draw people to you. Choose joy—dare to get out of your comfort zone and try new things. There's more out there if you just go for it. God has great things in store—be a person who refuses to settle for average.

GO FOR IT!

Sometimes we think if something is difficult, it must not be God's will or it would be easy. But we have a very powerful example to contradict that in the Bible. God said to the Israelites, "I have given you Canaan, now go out and take it!" God knew that the inhabitants of Canaan weren't going to welcome the Israelites and hand over their lands. It was going to be a battle.

If you want to be encouraged, read the story in the Book of Joshua about how the Israelites had to fight against all odds to take what God had promised. If God had given it to them why did they have to fight for it? The promises of God are not received automatically. Obedience and faith are required to obtain His promises.

God kept speaking to them over and over in these Scriptures about being strong and courageous. Here is one example:

> *Have I not commanded you? Be strong and courageous. Do not be terrified; do not be discouraged, for the Lord your God is with you wherever you go* (Joshua 1:9 NIV).

God wanted the Israelites to learn by experience that He was with them but they had to put faith into action. By following God's every command and fighting with the tenacity of a bulldog, they experienced miraculous victories over their enemies. Their enemies were ferocious and savage in their ways. Unless the Israelites learned how to hear God's voice and fight with His weapons, they would never have been able to maintain their victories.

Did you know that when a bulldog locks his jaw, it is almost impossible to wrench him loose? So it must be with us. It is in the effort, in the tenacity, in the struggle to accomplish our dreams in obedience to God's direction, that they really become ours. The end result is that through those battleground experiences we develop the godly wisdom that is required to handle the fulfillment and success of our dreams.

Unfortunately, too often we take the easy way out and settle for what is just OK. We're not really living out our dream, but what we are doing is attainable. It may not be the best we had hoped for, but it is good enough, it is OK. I really believe that God made us for more than "good enough."

Well, you may say, "I don't have the energy and strength I had when I was younger." True. But I do know from experience that when we are excited and enthused about something, we seem to have more energy. Like Emily discovered, life takes on a glow and we have a spring in our step and joy in our eyes when we move forward to fulfill our dream.

In writing this book, I have looked at the broken dreams and tragedies of my own life. While I had a wonderful, secure childhood; I have still had to deal with tragedies and devastation. I haven't always made the right choices. I haven't always walked in the wisdom of the Lord. I haven't always followed my dreams.

One of the more startling things I discovered in looking at my past life was made clear to me just recently. A new ministry was coming to our area and the leaders asked some people to recommend a woman who might be helpful in getting their ministry off the ground. They recommended me.

These men called and we met. I liked the two men who were in charge of the ministry, and what they needed was much of what I already did. They were looking for someone to help them gather people together, for someone to be a spokesperson for them. Because I believed in what they wanted to accomplish, at first I agreed to be part of their ministry.

But I found myself with sleepless nights. How was I going to fit in the additional responsibilities required to help them and still write this book. Finally, I had to tell them I couldn't be part of their ministry. It was so hard because I liked them and their wives a lot.

But the process of prayers and searching God brought me to a conclusion. I share this because I think many women have gone through their life doing what I've done.

When I married and then had children, I put aside my own dreams to be a wife and mom to my two boys. I believe this is a wise choice for women, because our children need us. But, when I found myself with an unwanted divorce,

173

shame, and disillusionment, I felt God let me down. I was mad at God and men.

Some years later when I met and then married my husband, Morry, I began writing for a Christian radio program as well as for magazines. At the time I thought God was leading me into Christian radio but instead, I ended up helping our pastor start his radio program. I handled his mailing list, wrote his partner letters and organized his fundraising dinners. I was helping someone else achieve their dream, making it possible for them to succeed.

Later, my husband and I helped launch a Christian TV station. Once more, I was helping others with their dream.

Then we helped a church get started in our area. I taught women's Bible studies, worked in the office and in the nursery. Because I was so busy, I stopped writing and speaking to women's groups for a time. Again, I was helping others to fulfill their dreams.

Do you see a pattern here? In searching my heart and searching God's will with this most recent offer for ministry, I realized it's easy for me to want to help others with their dreams and goals while mine are put on hold. To tell these wonderful men I couldn't help them was very difficult for me. But when I finally made the decision, it felt like a load of rocks had lifted off my shoulders. For once, I was choosing my dream instead of someone else's.

Your story may be a little different but in talking to women, I have found that pattern to be true for many of us. Because we are by nature "helpers," we put our own plans and dreams on hold for others. Sometimes it isn't only women who have given up their dreams for others. I have talked to some men who chose the vocation their parents wanted for them, rather than what they wanted. Their dreams were put aside too.

But now, as Savvy Singles, we can choose to fulfill *our* dreams. If your family history is one of mediocrity—rise above your family past, get a new image of yourself, look at your potential instead of your lack.

Years ago I heard a pastor say, *"The same power that raised Jesus from the dead resides in you!"* That truth often rumbles around in my spirit. If that same power does indeed reside in me, then I have no need for hesitation to follow my God-given dreams.

If you really believe that, then nothing can stop you from accomplishing all that God has for you. It's never too late! You can begin to take the first steps today. After all, you have resurrection power residing in you. God didn't put your dreams and talents in you for you to fail!

God's not limited by our background, lack of education, or family situation. He is only limited by our lack of faith and desire. Keep pursuing what is in your heart. Make a decision today to be what God wants you to be.

Part of that decision to be what God wants us to be is what is inside of us. Are we living and abiding in the fruit of the Spirit as we pursue our dreams? Do we truly walk in love, joy, and peace? Are we long-suffering? Do we have a passion for seeking God's wisdom in all of our decisions? As we learn to be creative and productive in these our Savvy

Single years, let's savor each moment of the process and ask God for wisdom.

Whether you want to be a clown, writer, teacher, poet, start your own new business, be a mentor to children, or have time to learn how to play the piano, the choice is yours. As a Savvy Single, you have more opportunities than you realize to fulfill your dream or dreams. If we desire, we can live a rich, passion-filled life with Christ as our guide.

As I mentioned previously, one of my favorite authors is Viktor Hugo, French poet, novelist and playwright. He expressed a limitless hope for his own future when he was more than 80 years old. He said, "Within my soul I feel the evidence of my future life. I am like a forest that has been cut down more than once, yet the new growth has more life than ever. I am always rising toward the sky with the sun shining on my head."

So, Savvy Singles, "We gotta get our fire back!" Remember, with God *all* things are possible. It's as we delight in the One who made us, who loves unconditionally, who knows every tear we shed, knows the number of hairs on our head, died to save us and desires His best for us, we can look to our future with hope. His desire is for us to maximize our potential.

By applying the powerful principles you've learned in this book, the best years of living are ahead. When we place our hand in His strong hand and allow Him to lead us down this new adventurous path He has for each one of us, the path of the Savvy Single, then we will realize our heart's desires and become all that He planned for us to be.

May the Son shine upon you as you seek and discover new realms of growth and possibilities!

As this book has come to an end, I have realized there hasn't been any room to explore friendships. However, I also realized that until we become healed and whole, we are not ready for godly relationships. So get ready for the next book to help you navigate the uncharted waters of dating in the singles' world of 50 and beyond!

POINTS TO PONDER

- ❖ Believe in impossible dreams.

- ❖ "God will make the impossible, possible in an impossible hour." Oral Roberts

- ❖ "If our dreams can be accomplished without God's help, then our dreams are too small."

- ❖ "If we are obedient, God will move the farthest star or the smallest grain of sand to help us." Oswald Chambers

- ❖ Even your tiniest step toward a dream can be powerful.

- ❖ Good enough is not good enough for you—a child of the Most High God.

- ❖ Your choices bring out the beauty of your soul.

- ❖ Get your fire back. Be enthusiastic. Choose joy. Try new things.

- ❖ The promises of God are achieved through obedience and faith.

- ❖ Through the struggle our dreams become real.

- ❖ Rise above your past—look at your potential.

- ❖ Learn to be creative and productive—savor each moment and ask God for wisdom.

AUTHOR'S RECOMMENDED READING LIST

❖ *Boundaries in Dating* by Drs. Cloud and Townsend

❖ *Committed but Flawed* by Cecil Murphey

❖ *Dream Seeds* by Mike Murdock

❖ *Intimate Prayer* by Dr. Lloyd Ogilvie

❖ *It's Time For Your Comeback* by Tim Storey

❖ *Men Are Like Waffles, Women Are like Spaghetti* by Bill & Pam Farrel

❖ *The Five Love Languages for Singles* by Gary Chapman

CALLING ALL SAVVY SINGLES

As this manuscript unfolded, it became obvious that much more needs to be said about Savvy Singles' issues than would fit in a single volume. This book was written for and by Savvy Singles, just like you and me. It's the real life stories and examples that allow us to laugh at ourselves and learn how to live more fulfilling and joyful lives.

That is why I am extending an invitation to you to share a brief (maximum 300 words) humorous or insightful story about living the life of a Savvy Single. Don't be concerned about your writing skills, we will edit it as needed.

Send your story to me by e-mail to:
Savvyseniors7@aol.com

Website:
www.samanthalandy.com

or address snail-mail to:

Samantha Landy
3104 East Camelback Rd., #851
Phoenix, AZ 85016

Be sure to include your contact information including address, e-mail, and phone numbers so I can get in touch in the event I select your story to be used in a future Savvy Singles publication. Stories will not be returned so be sure to retain a copy for your own files.

ABOUT THE AUTHOR

Life is the greatest teacher. Few people are willing to share with others those important life lessons learned—but then few people have heard the call as clearly as Samantha Landy.

Overflowing with rich and fascinating stories of lessons learned from walking with her Lord, Samantha's gift is a living well in the desert of life. Going where few have dared to tread, Samantha has taken her love of the Lord into country clubs, onto golf courses, homes for unwed mothers, shelters for abused women, and other such unlikely places to be His witness.

The one-of-a-kind ministry she founded in 1987, Christian Celebrity Luncheons, has hosted a dynamic list of Christian celebrities and has inspired and touched the lives of thousands of people. Whether talking about family, dating, relationships, death, divorce, and yes, loving, Samantha has tasted it all. Be dazzled, inspired, moved to tears and laughter, but also be ready to *be changed and challenged!*

Samantha is available to enrich your group with powerful presentations customized to your organization's needs.

Samantha serves on a number of national Christian boards such as the National Advisory Guideposts Cabinet, and is best known as an international conference and retreat speaker.

TV appearances include: "700 Club," "Back on Course," "The Hour of Healing," "TBN," "Talk of the Desert," as well as local and national TV.

Magazine articles have appeared in: *The Christian Communicator, Women's Aglow Magazine, Celebration, Haven of Rest, Guideposts,* and various other periodicals. Her nationally published weekly column is titled: "The Way...As I See It." Samantha's books include: *God's Creatures, Reflections, New Beginnings, Dining With Desert Celebrities, A Shalom Morning* (Devotional), *The Way...As I See It* (Devotional) and her latest, *The Savvy Singles Sabbatical Handbook.*

SAVVY SENIOR SABBATICALS

Savvy Senior Sabbaticals devotional book is a pot-pourri of the predicaments as well as promises of these, the best years of our lives. Join Samantha in learning to laugh about our forgetful foibles while we discover that failure is not fatal to the Savvy Senior who puts their trust in God. This is a book the "over fifty senior, men and women will want to keep by their bed as an inspiration before drifting off to sleep.

PSALMS FOR A SLEEPLESS NIGHT - CD

Have trouble going to sleep? Wake up in the night and can't get back to sleep? This new CD by Samantha is a reading of the Psalms with soft, soothing background music to not only relax and soothe your tired, stressed brain but nurture you and encourage you with God's Word. It is an hour long CD but so far, people who have used it never progress past the first 20 minutes. We guarantee, if this CD of Scripture doesn't put you to sleep, return it for a full refund!

DINING WITH DESERT CELEBRITIES

Would you like to know what you have in common with Christian Celebrities? Now you can take their photos, signatures, and favorite recipes right into your own kitchen with you, if you have a DINING WITH DESERT CELEBRITIES cookbook! From Carol Lawrence's Pasta E Fagioli on page 212, to the Cocoa-Pecan Pie of Adolph Coors IV on page 228, or the Lunar Bread from Astronaut Charlie Duke on page 40 and Gavin Mac Leod's World Class Eggplant recipe on page 88, this cookbook is simply the best there is!

Inside, you will find 23 other celebrity pictures, bios and recipes, including recipes from Mrs. Billy Graham and her daughters, Pat and DeDe Robertson, Oral and Evelyn Roberts, and others. On each index page there is also a devotional, to inspire you. Our desire was not only to also fill the tummy but to enrich the soul.

A SHALOM MORNING

Curl up in an easy chair and enjoy *A Shalom Morning*. Samantha's devotionals are often pictures of memories that will take you back in time to your own memories as she applies a thoughtful lesson for your contemplation. Below is one of the things her friends have written about *A Shalom Morning*. Enjoy!

"Samantha Landy's devotional is taken from her own experiences with God and with life. That's why you will benefit and be blessed by these essays, because her experiences are probably a lot like your own."

Cal Thomas,
Syndicated columnist, Fox News

THE WAY...AS I SEE IT

"Globe-trotter. Conference Speaker. Funny lady. Writer Samantha Landy shoehorns her devotionals full of travel information, notes from celebrities, and warm humor. In addition, she consistently applies a timeless thought that makes "The Way...As I See It" truly Samantha and worth reading and rereading."

Michael Ray Smith, PhD., Chair,
Campbell University
Dept. of Mass Communication

4-MINUTE MEDITATIONS

TODAY GOD IS FIRST

4-MINUTE MEDITATIONS
on the more important things in life

Os Hillman

TODAY GOD IS FIRST

Os Hillman has the uncanny ability to write just to my circumstance, exactly to my need. He helps me see from God's view. He strengthens my faith and courage to both see God and invite Him into the everyday trials and struggles of work.

So take this book to work; put it on your desk or table. Every day, just before you tackle the mountains before you, pause long enough to remind your self, Today, God is First.

ISBN 0-7684-2119-5

Available at your local Christian bookstore.

Additional copies of this book and other
book titles from DESTINY IMAGE are
available at your local bookstore.

For a bookstore near you, call 1-800-722-6774.

Send a request for a catalog to:

Destiny Image® Publishers, Inc.
P.O. Box 310
Shippensburg, PA 17257-0310

*"Speaking to the Purposes of God for This
Generation and for the Generations to Come"*

**For a complete list of our titles,
visit us at www.destinyimage.com**